Going Vertical

the life of an extreme kayaker

by Tao Berman
with Pam Withers

"Berman is the best-known kayaker on the planet."

—Sports Illustrated

Going Vertical

the life of an extreme kayaker

by Tao Berman
with Pam Withers

MENASHA RIDGE PRESS

All rights reserved
Published by Menasha Ridge Press
Printed in the United States of America
Distributed by Publishers Group West
First edition, first printing

Cover design by Travis Bryant
Text design by Annie Long
Cover photograph by Jock Bradley
Black-and-white photographs: Jock Bradley, pages 5, 56, and 142;
    all others courtesy of Tao Berman
Indexing by Rich Carlson

 Printed on recycled paper

Library of Congress Cataloging-in-Publication Data

    Berman, Tao, 1979–
        Going vertical: the life of an extreme kayaker/by Tao Berman
    with Pam Withers.
        p. cm.
        ISBN-13: 978-0-89732-652-0
        ISBN-10: 0-89732-652-0
        1. Kayaking. I. Withers, Pam. II. Title.
        GV783.B47 2008
        797.122′4092—dc22
        [B]
                        2008011674

Menasha Ridge Press
P.O. Box 43673
Birmingham, Alabama 35243
www.menasharidge.com

table *of* contents

*"If there is magic on this planet,
it is contained in water."*

—Loren Eiseley,
anthropologist, environmentalist, and poet

REDEFINING LIMITS

"The paradox is that we're born with two conflicting instincts: one designed to protect us from gravity, the other urging us to play with it."

—Garrett Soden, *Falling*

Picture a long, steeply sloped slide of stone shaped like a lightning bolt, resting in the rain forests of British Columbia. Sloped at roughly a sixty-degree angle, it nestles at its upper end against the island's snow-covered hills. Its bottom section is washed by salty waves. In springtime, a shallow chute of water rushes down the top of this wall from snowmelt to sea. The moment I saw this natural waterslide while cruising western Canada's rugged coast in a Zodiac, I knew that when spring next hit and fed a more substantial tongue of water down it, I would be back.

Why? Because I live for pushing limits. I'm a professional whitewater kayaker known for first descents of waterfalls and difficult sections of river. I hold three world records for this, including one of the two Guinness-recognized waterfall descents at 98.4 feet. I've also done more than fifty first descents of steep, boulder-choked rivers and have been a Pre-Worlds champion for freestyle whitewater kayaking. So when I first saw this mind-blowing natural rockslide, I knew I had to kayak it.

Kayaking waterfalls and rivers all over the world is an unusual way to make a living, I admit. But even if NBC and *Sports Illustrated* hadn't been willing to rent a helicopter and jet boats to station two dozen camera operators, producers, and assistants, plus a sports host, around the drop the day I tackled it, I would still have returned to this site.

Rationally, I know it doesn't make sense to put my life on the line for my chosen sport, but I can't help it. It's what I love; it's a sort of addiction I don't want to kick. And there's got to be a reason I've never injured myself in fifteen years of pushing the envelope. It's more than luck. It's setting goals that may look impossible to others and training so hard that I'm measuring risks from a different realm than those shaking their heads in dismay or disapproval. It's honing my instincts until they are trained reactions and surrounding myself with talented help.

The rock wall I've just described is called Lacy Falls, and it's roughly an hour's boat ride from the nearest town on Vancouver Island. As I stand on it three hundred feet up from the water—my kayak resting on my shoulder, my neoprene boots seeking solid footing—I breathe in the smell of pine trees and salt water. At the base of the falls, men hip-deep in the water are moving barnacle-covered rocks out of my intended water landing zone. Camera operators and still photographers are stationing themselves all around the rain-forest-choked wall. Also at the falls' base, three large boats and a helicopter hover. I spot the doctor that the television network insisted on sending, perched on a rock beside my landing pool just in case things don't go well. Before focusing on the descent, I reflect on how fortunate I am to get paid to be doing exactly what I like to do.

Lacy Falls is a solid slab of granite about fifty feet wide. It has flakes of rock embedded along its top. Unlike at water park slides, the water dashing down its surface is seasonal. The hill on which the wall is set accumulates only a small cap of snow in winter. So even in a record snow-fall year, the snowmelt sends no more than a shallow stream down the falls' length, and then for only a few weeks before it slows to a trickle. By summer, the waterslide is dry.

Then there's the beach waiting to greet this water spill. The moon's pull dictates when the sea beneath the falls is less than two feet deep and when it reaches a depth of ten feet. Meanwhile, the surges of water that batter the shore have their own strange timing for tossing ice-cold water at the cliff base.

So for me, getting down this stony zigzag alive is all about timing. I want the maximum flow of water down its spine to cover the surface's rock flakes, which could otherwise spin me sideways, then onto my head. Or they could turn me into a human barrel rolling painfully down the face of the falls. And I want the maximum amount of water waiting for me at the bottom to soften the impact of hitting it at an estimated fifty miles per hour and to cover those barnacle-covered rocks, which could cause death or an unpleasant facial makeover if I land upside down.

I've also calculated that just before I go airborne above the steepest section—the wall's slope varies from fifty to eighty degrees—I need to turn my kayak sideways in order to ensure that I land in the ocean on my side, preventing me from plunging too deeply into my three-foot-deep landing pool.

I lift my kayak off my shoulder and place it on a rock beside the slide. I'm now three hundred feet above the water, and five hundred feet below the snowcap. (I've deemed the section above me too treacherous to try.) So that's three hundred feet I'll be traveling, perhaps the last twenty-five feet of it through the air.

Like most athletes, I do some warm-up exercises to get the blood flowing. I know I'm going to slap hard into the water below the falls, and I know I can minimize injury by warming up properly. Next, I visualize my route and the moves I must make—for something like the thirtieth time. If I build up too much momentum, I remind myself, I will land on exposed rocks to the left of my landing pool. If I fail to build up enough momentum, I will hit rocks to the right of it. If I hit the middle of the pool as I plan, my left shoulder and side will absorb the impact, along with the left side of my kayak. I know it's going to be painful even if everything

goes right. But the only other options are splatting onto the rocks to either side of the falls or hurtling vertically into only three feet of water, which will likely injure me so badly I may never walk again.

The producer climbs up to where I'm standing and asks me if I'm sure I want to do it. The crew is seriously worried about this descent. I reply yes, I do, and I refuse to let the question shake me. I've been asked this question on many occasions before a big drop.

It's midafternoon, and the sun is bearing down. I know that for every half hour I wait, snowmelt above is spilling a little more water down my runway, covering those nasty rock flakes. On the other hand, the longer I wait, the more the tide below is pulling water out of my already-shallow landing pool.

I'm flirting with disaster on both ends; I must compromise. I eye the torrent and decide the time is now. I hear over the radio that safety crew, camera operators, sports host, and photographers are ready. I do one last visualization. I feel no fear or pressure. That may sound strange, but it's the way I always feel when about to run a big drop. I believe that fear comes from doubt, and if I doubted my abilities to kayak this falls, I wouldn't be here. I'm totally focused on the moves I need to make.

I take a deep, steadying breath. I step into my kayak and attach my spray deck. I press my feet tightly against the boat's bulkhead so that if I crash into a rock, my ankles will absorb maximum impact before they break, if they must break. Then I give a thumbs-up letting everyone know I'm about to go.

Whoosh! I'm off. The actual feat takes only about eight seconds, but for me, time is immaterial. I'm immediately aware that my speed is exponentially higher than I had planned. The water is so clear directly under my kayak's bottom that I can see the rock flakes hurtling past underneath me. At this speed, even a one-inch flake can launch me off this rock wall.

Soon, a two-inch flake decides to test me. It tries to turn me sideways as it scrapes my kayak's bottom.

I put in a hard left rudder stroke, determined to keep my bow down and reorient the boat to its straight-ahead position. Doing so in shallow water is difficult. I press my paddle so hard against the bottom that I can hear it screeching against rock. Just as I succeed in straightening myself out, I hit a larger flake. The hit compresses my entire kayak and body, and I know instinctively that it's going to launch me like a ski jump. Before it spits me into the air, I manage to lean to the left, hoping I can still make my landing pool.

I'm flying up, up, and over the last and steepest portion of the falls with a left spin. I end up shooting through thirty feet of air, thanks to that second stone flake, which was maybe three inches high. It turns out I have enough momentum to not only clear the bottom of the falls, but also to sail past my target landing point. In other words, my premature start has messed up my ability to land where I had planned. As the water approaches at a dizzying speed, I hope I haven't miscalculated how hard I'm going to land or what the potential consequences would be of hitting under-surface rocks.

Whack! I land on my side as I had hoped, a little farther out than my ideal spot, but still in the deepest part of the water. I feel my entire rib cage start to implode on impact. I've experienced this sensation before; I just hope that the pressure stops before my ribs break. So far, it always has.

The landing knocks the wind out of me as my kayak enters no more than two feet of water. What have I done to myself? I wonder as the kayak capsizes. I'm now upside down in the shallow seawater, trying to roll up with my paddle. Each time I try to roll upright, the kayak spins back upside down, as unstable as a floating log under a logger's boots.

Clearly, something is wrong. I assume I've injured myself badly, and I expect the pain to kick in any second. But I need to roll up to breathe. As I set up under water to roll again, I can feel rocks pressing against the back of my life jacket and knocking into my helmet.

Finally, I roll up successfully and paddle unsteadily to shore as safety crew members rush toward me. I look down to see that the left side of my kayak is crushed in three-quarters of a foot, like a beer can someone has jumped on. No wonder I had difficulty rolling up! As I run my fingers over the dent, I realize soberly that the landing exerted the same pressure on my shoulder and rib cage. I move my fingers gently to my side. Just a tender touch makes me wince. But, bruised or broken, it doesn't really matter to me at that moment. What matters is that I've survived; I reacted properly to the early launch and hit the water near where I'd planned. I pulled it off. I realize I've done it as I sit breathing hard at the bottom of the falls. It's a moment I savor. It's the reason I kayak.

Crew members are trying to help me out of my kayak. They congratulate me with worried expressions.

"Are you okay, Tao? Are you sure you're okay?"

"Just sore," I report, hoping this will prove to be true. Experience has taught me that it takes twenty-four hours to judge the extent of an injury. Soreness one day can mean fiery pain the next. But I can handle that; I don't want anyone fussing over me now. Safety-crew members draw relieved breaths, and the camera operators tell me they've captured excellent footage.

Perfect, I think. The television network is happy, sponsors are happy, the crew is happy, and I'm stoked, because for eight seconds, I pushed the limits while striving for perfection, and pulled it off.

I don't get a helicopter ride. I have to take the jet boat to the harbor. But I don't mind because it gives me time to celebrate with crew members, some of whom are my closest friends. Later, after accepting another round of congratulations and downing a big meal at a local diner, I call it a night. The next morning I awake barely sore at all. Lucky, for sure. But for me, that kind of luck is always melded with weeks of preparation and years of honing my boating instincts.

I run waterfalls, rapids, and extreme kayak races for a living because they provide the ultimate challenge. I'm putting everything on the line. One mistake, and I'm dead or seriously injured. I'm not interested in killing myself, so for me it has to be a calculated risk. I spend hours exploring a falls that I'm considering paddling—visualizing, deciding if I have the skills to tackle it and, if so, exactly how and where to run it. I've walked away from more than one falls I've judged would kill me. But once I've decided something is doable, it's all calculation, not emotion; nothing and no one can stop me. Fear is never part of the equation, especially not as I climb into my kayak at the cusp of a falls.

My successful run of Lacy Falls didn't win any world records, and its splash in the news media was short-lived. That's okay by me because world records are not what I'm all about. I live to kayak, and I kayak to live. This is my story.

CHILD OF CHALLENGE

"I'm far more afraid of being stifled, bored, and trapped in the cages they call buildings than I am of dying. I want to live, really live."

—Kirsten Kremer, Alaskan mountain guide and writer

What I remember most about growing up on a mountaintop in eastern Washington State are the tall, graceful aspens. On summer nights, they'd silhouette the moon above the ground tarp on which my mother, my older sister, Lilly, my younger brother, Osho, and I would sleep to the throb of crickets and frogs. In winter, I'd survey the trees' elegant white coats from where I pressed my nose against the window of our 500-square-foot converted barn before I'd rush out and shake them with glee.

But best of all was my childhood game of tree tag. That's when friends and I would climb up and jump between the trees, often hurling ourselves from one branch to another twenty feet above the ground. Anyone who touched the ground was "it." Sometimes the strong but flexible

Lilly

I was four years older, but we had a lot of the same friends because we were in a small-knit community. Tao was lots of fun—always going, going, going. He was a total energy ball, more so than any of us. He wasn't one to sit out or be calm. He was extremely bright and always kind. We were taught to treat others as we wanted to be treated. We were all good kids. There wasn't a lot to get in trouble with—not a lot to do except play outside with each other.

branches would bend. You'd climb up them, swing on them, and then they'd gently lower you to the ground. Once in a while, of course, they'd snap. Then we'd find ourselves lying on the ground with a piece of tree on top of us. Even if that inflicted pain, however, it would never stop us from climbing right back up into the trees. We played for hours upon hours in the trees as my mother chopped wood, drew water from a nearby stream, chased our free-run chickens, or gathered herbs from the surrounding forest and her garden.

My parents were true back-to-the-earth hippies. My mother—the oldest of six children who'd grown up in a middle-class family in Seattle, Washington—acquired a degree in psychology from the University of

Washington before traveling the world. She hitchhiked across the Sahara Desert and lived in an oasis for a while. During her time in Africa, she learned to walk carrying loads on her head and marveled at the way young children there and in other developing countries were given responsibility and independence from a very young age. This, she observed, gave them an assured confidence long before Western children.

When she returned to the United States, she decided to reject materialism and stifling city life. She changed her name from Pam Johnson to Silvermoon, the name an African medicine man had given her. She moved to a wickiup (a domed shelter of saplings and canvas) on a remote mountaintop. There, she gave birth to "Raspberry" (my sister changed her name to Lilly when she was four) and spent her days "learning the lessons that the earth and its seasons teach." (That's a quote from a February 27, 1977, *Seattle Times* magazine article about her.) Her community included five families that shared frequent social get-togethers and, most importantly to her, values. Her own parents were upset at her chosen lifestyle, but she was totally committed to it.

She met my father, Birch (his original name was Steve), when Lilly was three and he was delivering bulk foods to the families on the mountain. Reserved and intellectual, he was the son of a well-to-do Jewish family on Long Island, New York. His father was a well-known neurosurgeon, and his mother was a psychology professor. According to Mom, Dad was "clearly enamored" of the community. Shortly after they fell for each other, I was conceived. My mom says the relationship was shaky even before I was born, but they didn't split up until Osho was two. Even then, they tried to work things out until my mother was expecting Colin, who ended up being raised by another family in the community.

Mom claims she knew she was in for an energetic child months before I was born. She says I was unlike any of my siblings, before or after birth. Shortly before I arrived, she decided I was like a hyperactive dolphin "diving, twisting, twirling, swimming" inside her. She also says that after I was born, unlike her other babies, I never let her put me down for

15

Mom

I carried all my babies in a special carrier on my back so I could chop wood, fetch water, gather vegetables from the garden, or walk or ride my horse ten miles into town. I was used to working really hard— weeding and building fences, for example, in return for staying on our plot of land. As long as I kept moving, I could do anything.

We moved outside in summer, and we'd be there all morning, bathing the kids in a washtub, reading, and making breakfast around our campfire. We'd take care of their every need. I felt like my kids were completely fulfilled.

When Tao started crawling, we had difficulty catching him. That quickly developed into a game. He'd crawl as fast as he could off our wood platform toward the goats, laughing and knowing we'd chase him. We made a gate, and sometimes he'd even manage to get through that. He would also climb anything he could find. I spent a lot of time at the bottom of ladders.

I remember when Tao and Osho were toddlers, walking up the hill to our house with the two of them hanging onto my skirt between pushing, tussling, and tumbling like squirrels, always trying to get ahead of each other, these two little balls of activity.

Tao loved to make us laugh. After every meal he'd put his bowl over his head whether it was empty or not. He didn't eat much because he was too busy to eat. He'd scarf down his food and leap away to do something. Put a child like him into a typical school, and he'll be called hyperactive. My perception was that he had a lot of energy moving through him—wonderful, clean energy.

Birch was very communicative with Tao when Tao was a tiny child. He engaged Tao in long discussions. I was never that verbal. I was a real physical person, doing arts and crafts, exploring, playing hide-and-seek and kick the can with them. I homeschooled my kids as long as I could. I didn't want to put Tao in school and torture him and the teachers. When my kids did go to school, I missed being able to watch their minds grow and blossom and open. Tao started at public school in the middle part of first grade. I let his teachers know he had a lot of energy—that was part of who he was. He managed to survive those teachers, and they survived him.

a minute and demanded independence way earlier than any other child she'd ever known.

Sorry, Mom, but it's not like I remember any of that. My father wanted to name me Barley, so I feel lucky my mom chose Tao (pronounced *Tay*-o), which means "universal energy." For me, of course, growing up with tons of freedom and instant access to the outdoors was idyllic. Days were filled with exploring the woods and jumping off boulders into the Kettle River. We all learned to swim at a young age.

Osho was my best playmate and closest friend. We used to ride our one-speed bikes everywhere, tearing down our mountain at high speed, crashing spectacularly, and then doing it all again. My bike's most prominent features were back brakes and a chain that fell off as much as it stayed on. Unfortunately, when the chain fell off, I had no brakes, which meant I crashed big. With no television or radio, we also played endless card games of go fish and rummy.

One winter when I was four, I found a pair of old skis, the kind you had to tie on by winding straps around your ankles. I practiced skiing in our little driveway. Mom remembers me being totally absorbed in teaching myself skiing for two hours at a time on those things, my legs wobbling all the way down. When I reached the end of the driveway, I had to undo the skis, trek back up the hill, fix them onto me again, and then do it all over.

When I was around five, Osho and I were biking down a dirt road together and came to a herd of cattle. Their tails swished at flies, and their hooves crunched against the gravel. Osho and I wrinkled our noses against their distinct bovine smell. It never occurred to us to get off our bikes and skirt them. We just ploughed right down the middle of the moving herd, pumping our pedals the way a cowboy might kick his boot

18

The barn we lived in until I was ten years old. In summer, Mom would set
up an outdoor camp near our barn.

heels against his horse's sides. The cattle parted for us with no more than curious glances as Mom half freaked out behind us.

It was actually rare that I wasn't in pain from some bike crash. At ten, I was biking as fast as I could, pushing those pedals like pistons, feeling beads of sweat form on my forehead. Then my baseball cap slid down because of the sweat and covered my eyes. No! Everything went dark. Before I could raise a hand from my handlebar to shove the cap back up, my bike wobbled beneath me, and I flew off the road. Body tensed for the crash, I careered ten feet down into a ditch, where my head bashed so hard it felt like something had risen from the ground to punch it. A rock, as it turned out, had penetrated my skull. Sticky blood ran into my face. I looked down at my arms to see they were all torn up. *No worries,* I told myself gravely; *I'm right near a neighbor's house.*

"Hey, George," I said when he answered my knock at the door. "Can you fix me up?"

Old George scratched his head as he looked me over and frowned.

"How about I fetch your mom?" he suggested.

"No!" I objected quickly. "I mean, please just help me clean up a little? If she sees me like this, she'll make me wear a helmet."

I had countless scrapes and tumbles in childhood, as would anyone living in the outdoors with tons of freedom to play. Ironically, however, I have yet to suffer a major injury in almost fifteen years of extreme kayaking. Perhaps a childhood of freedom to explore limits and perfect the art of calculating risks continues to stand me in good stead.

Our mountain community wasn't a formal commune, but the people there supported each other and got together a lot. Among these was George, the old guy who lived just up the mountain from us. We called

Osho

Being Tao's little brother was a real pain in the ass. He was hard to beat at anything; he was a tough one. He just hates losing. I can beat him at a few things now, so I'm pretty happy about that. But he's still good at almost anything he does.

him "Grandpa George." Grandpa George used to give Lilly, Osho, and me food that Mom or Dad didn't, including graham crackers and macaroni and cheese. Once, when I was six, Mom got curious when, for the third day in a row, Osho and I politely (we thought) turned down the breakfast she'd made for us and asked to be excused to race away up the hill. She followed us and arrived at George's doorstep just in time to see the two of us sitting happily on each side of him, plates stacked high with pancakes. I can still conjure up the smell and taste of those pancakes, each with a huge chunk of butter and a heap of peanut butter and strawberry jam. At the time, Osho and I looked at each other and said, "Oh-oh." Luckily, Mom just laughed.

Another member of the community lived not far down the hill. His name was Snowquiet. He had a berry patch he tended so carefully that Osho and I had to develop great stealth to sneak in and eat to our hearts' content. When I was six, Osho and I were walking up the grassy trail from a berry raid one morning. Our mouths purple with berry juice, our tummies happily gurgling, we were probably licking our lips and exchanging

Lilly

I remember berry picking with Tao and Mom and Osho when Tao was around eight. Tao would put one berry in his bucket and eat like five, put another in the pail and eat a couple more. He finally ended up with one little pail full of berries. When we went to weigh in, Mom told the cashier, "We have to pay more because Tao ate a whole bunch." Tao's like, "Mom, why would you tell them that?" Mom was like, "You have to be honest." In the end, the place didn't make Mom pay more. Tao sure loved berries. Still does.

satisfied smiles when we came to a fork in the trail. Our sneakers stopped dead as we gazed up into the face of a towering black bear. Pulse quickening, I reached for Osho's hand and did exactly what you're not supposed to do: I raced up the right-hand trail at high speed, Osho in tow. I glanced around once, just long enough to see that the bear appeared just as anxious to get away from us. He sniffed, lowered his front paws back to the dirt, now marked by our shoe prints, and took off to the left.

A few minutes later, I was panting a little as I approached another fork, half-dragging Osho behind me. "Oh-oh!" I shouted to my little brother as my heart sank. There was that same bear, lumbering toward us where his trail rejoined ours. This time I bent down, picked up a rock, and threw it at the big animal. Then, heart pounding but proud of my bravery, I grabbed Osho's hand again and raced even faster for our house.

Besides all our outdoor activities, we read a lot, encouraged especially by Dad, who was always correcting my grammar and engaging me in worldly discussions. I remember reading all the Hardy Boys series—at a rate of one per night. They perfectly captured my sense of adventure and made me a reader for life. Likewise, my Grandma Doreen, Dad's mother, made sure we read a lot when we visited her. Because we had no television at home, Osho and I were pretty keen to watch one at Grandma's house during our visits to Great Neck, New York. But her rule was that we had to read for as many minutes as we watched television.

Grandma Doreen was the best grandma in the world, very supportive, always interested in what we were doing and not judgmental about my parents' lifestyle (at least not to us). She also loved to spoil us. Knowing we had so little in Washington, she took us on annual shopping trips for clothes and toys. But if we got forward enough to list what we wanted, she'd let us know that wasn't "proper."

Grandma Doreen

When Tao was around five, he required a medical procedure that necessitated him to lie totally still for thirty minutes or else be anesthetized. The doctors discussed it, then asked Tao if he thought he could keep still. He said yes, and by God he did it. Everyone was astonished that a child of that age could concentrate like that, could keep such an intense focus.

Once a year, Osho and I would fly across the country by ourselves to visit her and Grandpa, even when I was only six and Osho was four and a half. Officially, of course, we had an airline escort between Dad's drop-off and Grandma's pickup. But, as Grandma keenly remembers, Osho and I would rush off the plane to greet her, unlike our cousins, who would arrive hand firmly in hand with the airline personnel.

Grandma's lifestyle so contrasted with ours that it was an eye-opener for us, not that we were overly conscious of it when we were young. As toddlers, we'd tear around her finely appointed house on a plastic tricycle as she smiled with gritted teeth. We also played endless rounds of baseball in the backyard with her and Grandpa.

Once, when I was eight and Osho was seven, Grandma took us and two cousins through a nature preserve in Florida. She was pretty flustered trying to keep four small grandchildren in sight at all times, and she panicked big-time when she turned around at one point and I wasn't there. She looked north, south, east, and west, her panic growing. Then she

Lilly

Once, our maternal grandmother came to stay for a couple of days and brought a cooked ham with her. She thought it would last the entire visit. But Tao loved it so much he kept eating it and eating it until it was all gone the first night. We just didn't get that type of food. She couldn't believe it.

spotted me high in a tree above—so high that she was afraid to call me down for fear I'd hurt myself. When I finally landed on the ground, entirely pleased with myself, she admonished me never to do that again.

Growing up in our isolated community never really gave me a sense that we were poor, despite the visits to New York. I didn't know any differently. There was always food on the table, so I never really gave a thought to how little money my parents had. Especially after Mom and Dad separated, Mom was pretty challenged to look after us all. There were years her income totaled four thousand dollars (from picking fruit in nearby orchards, among other tasks). Even with land in return for work, and a garden and chickens that fed us much of the year, that was a stretch. On the other hand, we didn't have the kind of everyday bills other families had. We had no electricity or car, so there were no electricity, car insurance, or gas bills. Mom home-schooled us for a while, but even when she started sending us to school, she did whatever it took to allow for school-clothes shopping before we started.

Every four months, Mom would use the community truck to fetch staples like flour and lentils from the nearest town. If we wanted to visit friends, we had to walk there and back—preferably before dark. There was no hot water. A shower was a bucket of cold water over the head. When we wanted to eat, we'd have to build the fire and help pluck the chicken. When we wanted a new toy, we'd have to bike down to town and sell our old toys to raise money for it.

I learned not to wait for things to come to me. I went out and worked to make things happen. To this day, those lessons remain firmly embedded. When I want something, I just go after it until I get it. I believe in yes; I can't handle no. I suppose on occasion this gets me into trouble, but I think it has helped me achieve what I want more often than it has hurt me.

Even in sixth grade, when I sold candy door-to-door, I earned thirteen dollars an hour. At age eleven, I sold a selection of old toys in front of a grocery store in order to earn enough to buy a remote-control car that cost $150, a fortune by our family's standards. Whereas other kids scarfed all their Halloween candy the week of Halloween, I saved mine until my friends had run out, then sold mine to them. When other kids wanted to buy something, they just asked their parents. I didn't have that luxury. I learned at a very young age that money doesn't grow on trees, that earning it requires creative thinking and hard work. I had to depend on myself. While some might think that reflects poorly on my parents, I believe the opposite is true: The self-sufficiency their circumstances taught me has been invaluable.

Like me, Lilly regards our upbringing as idyllic, even though the two of us agree we would never raise our own kids that way. Osho has a harsher view of the hippie upbringing. One thing I really respect about Mom, though, is that she did a good job at making sure we had whatever we needed. She always put our best interests first; she did whatever needed to be done for us, somehow.

Dad was a great dad in his own way. He didn't compromise his values at all. If he felt that someone had done something wrong, he'd cut that person out of his life even if it was a detriment to Osho and me. He's set in his ways; it's either his way or nothing. He's also analytical and risk averse. What I got from him is my calculated approach and (Mom says) my business skills. He expected me to speak correctly and present myself well; those are other valuable tools he gave me. I hated it when he corrected me as a child, but now I really appreciate that he did so. Although he wrestled in high school, I wouldn't describe him as competitive, and he certainly doesn't take unnecessary risks. You'd hardly know I was his son in that sense. He's a

Dad and me

laid-back, mellow guy. He looks at each thing as if there is a lesson to be learned from it. That was hard to deal with as a kid, but it helped make me who I am today. Also, Dad never gave us an allowance. Instead, he paid us to do pull-ups. Every time we broke our previous record, we would get a bonus.

Dad

In wintertime, when Tao was a baby and until he was about two, I would rise as soon as it was light and bundle him up, and we'd go outside. We'd sit for an hour, hanging out in the snow, huddled up and enjoying ourselves. These are fond memories.

In contrast, my mother's family is full of athletes. She herself was a competitive diver in high school, even beating someone who shortly afterward went on to the Olympics.

After my parents split up, my mother lived on one mountain and my father lived on another, where he developed a wilderness-guide business using donkeys. By then, I was going to school in a nearby town—walking or hitchhiking to a friend's house to catch a ride down the mountain to the school-bus stop. After school, if I wanted to return home to Mom, I took one bus. If I felt like seeing Dad, I'd take a different one. There was no formal arrangement such as "weekends with Dad," but I ended up on his mountain several days a week.

I have perhaps one memory of my mother and father being in the same room together and not fighting. In fact, after I turned four, pretty much the only time I saw them together was during attempted family-counseling sessions. I find it pretty hypocritical that these two people were living a hippie, off-the-grid lifestyle promoting world peace but

I was raised in the metropolitan New York area. My choices were obviously different from my parents' and siblings'. My father had a great deal of trouble with it earlier on, my mother less so. At this point, they've both been very accepting of my different choices for a long time.

couldn't even speak to one another. That made things difficult for my brother and me. Sometimes, as a child, you feel pretty lost when you're hearing two different stories from your parents.

These days, I'd say my dad and I are close in some ways and not in others. We speak on the phone perhaps every two weeks. In all three years that I've lived only six hours away from him, however, he's visited me only once, and that was for a day. Once, I was kind of curious how long it would take him to call me if I didn't call him. It took two months. Still, in our own way we're close.

When I was a child, Mom always told me to have confidence in myself. I took that to heart. Confidence is built on success, and my parents gave us plenty of opportunities to make our own success. To this day, if I make a mistake, I always redo whatever I was doing until I'm successful. I hate to fail. I've been that way my entire life.

EXTREME TEEN

"The river is always restless. Even in its gentle moods, it is hungry, forever tugging at whatever is in reach."

—Bill Thomas,
American Rivers: A Natural History

t was a spring evening, and I was ten years old. Mom sat us down around the only table in our mountaintop dwelling—the renovated barn that had neither electricity nor running water. She turned up the kerosene lantern. Her blue eyes and uncharacteristically serious face scanned Lilly, Osho, and me in turn.

Uh-oh, I thought, trying not to fiddle. *Family sit-down time, and something's up.*

"Okay," she began, "I want to know what you kids want."

Lilly, fourteen going on twenty, didn't bother raising her hand or consulting with her little brothers. To her mind, this was her big chance. "We want electricity," she declared, tossing her hair and narrowing her eyes at Mom. She always was assertive, our big sister Lilly.

Mom turned to Osho and me. We shrugged our shoulders and grinned. We didn't care. We were just along for the ride, so to speak, in this adventuresome life.

"Well then," Silvermoon concluded, smiling. "I guess it's time to show you the world."

And so it was that we packed all our worldly possessions into the ancient car we'd recently acquired—a dented-up Subaru more suited to a junk heap than the backcountry roads of Washington. (For years, Lilly, Osho, and I would ask to be dropped off a few blocks away from our destination for fear someone would see us in it.) Mom hadn't decided exactly where we'd live next, but while we were driving through California, she was pretty taken with Heartwood, a community north of San Francisco known for its healing center. When we pulled in there, Osho and I spotted the swimming pool filled with kids and lost no time bailing out of the car and hopping into the water. As we splashed about, Mom was looking

Osho and me during a family road-trip. Notice me hanging off the cliff—I've always liked heights.

Osho

For the longest time when we were young, Tao wanted to be a used-car salesman. He really liked the idea of that.

around kind of starry-eyed, saying, "We could live here. I could get a job cooking, maybe, and get registered as a massage therapist." Then she scratched her head and said, "Where's Lilly?"

"Still in the car," Osho and I shouted. Why our big sister would sit in our overstuffed car in eighty-degree heat was beyond Osho's and my comprehension. But we tagged along back to the car, dripping, when Mom motioned us to follow her. There was Lilly, arms crossed and lower lip stuck out, with all the car's doors locked.

"We're not going to move here!" she declared, her eyes flashing at our startled mom. "I'm not unlocking the doors until you agree we're driving on. I'm tired of hippies!"

Mom heaved a big sigh and hugged us. "Lilly's right," she said. "This is about you now, not me. We'll keep driving." Hardly were we back in the car and snaking down a long hill when the car's brakes overheated. Mom, coolly working the hand brake to get us back to the highway, said, "Well, this car is trying to tell us something. We're not meant to live in California." So northward we headed, all the way back to Washington. And all too soon, we settled into a house near the bottom of our mountain, moving a year later to the small town of Monroe, Washington.

By then, I'd changed my name from Tao to Cody, inspired by the westerns I'd been reading about a manly daredevil named Wild Bill Cody. Neither Mom nor Dad could object, of course, given that both of them had changed their names.

As Cody, I found myself none too impressed with the real world as it pertained to fifth grade in Monroe. For years, I'd had no television or radio, so I was somewhat out of step with what was "cool." Teachers seemed unimpressed with the wise-guy jokes I was cracking in class, even if most of the kids liked them. I had confidence to burn, physical prowess to demonstrate, and a total inability to back down from a challenge. This led me into regular fistfights in no time. I remember learning early on not to drink out of a water fountain in the school halls for fear someone would smash my head into it. If someone pushed me, I'd push back. Then the guy would start throwing punches at me, I'd throw some back, and soon we'd be in an all-out brawl. Once, the police showed up for me at school. Sometimes the school would contact Mom, and then I'd be in hot water—the very luxury, if I can pun, for which we'd moved down the mountain.

Middle school was the worst period of my life. I hated it. Every day I'd wake up and dread going to school. Everyone seemed to be aligned with a clique, and they all were trying to be someone they weren't. To walk across the school grounds alone meant one was a loner. Cool kids would never talk to uncool kids, and so on. To my mind, it was all just plain dumb, and where I see similar cliques and behavior among paddling factions today, I have equal disdain for it. About the only thing I remember liking was the fighting. It was a way to test myself. I hated the bullies who picked on the wimpy kids. I would go out of my way to start fights with the bullies. Having fought throughout my school years, I was a tough kid; I lost only one fight.

I did well in all my classes. I just didn't like them. So perhaps two things saved me from going down a very dark road the next few years: first, the wrestling program I joined in seventh and eighth grades, and second, Mom's efforts to keep me occupied and away from trouble. I should add that a year into our lives in Monroe, Dad sacrificed much to move near us in order to be a larger part of Osho's and my lives. When we were kids, he'd take us to downhill-skiing areas on occasion, which was a real treat because we usually had to hike up if we wanted to ski down.

I was eleven when I agreed to help our Monroe landowner and friend, Jerin, move logs by crane. Jerin, a man I respected a great deal, was at the crane switches. He'd swing the crane's boom around and wait until I secured a large strap around a log. Then he'd swoop the log up into the air, turn it 180 degrees, and lower it to a pile. After a few hours of this, I asked him if I could get a carnival-style ride on the unloaded boom as he maneuvered it across the grassy patch of land. He said sure. It was quite a thrill to be lifted high into the air with nothing to secure me but my handhold on the loop in the rope dangling from the end of the boom. I probably yahooed once or twice before things went wrong. First, my weight started the empty boom swinging like a pendulum. As it swung out farther and farther, Jerin's face turned grim, and he shouted, "Hold on!"

That's the last thing I remember. Later, I was told that the rope swung so high that it slackened and then snapped tight again, which threw me at the ground. I held tightly to the strap, but by the rope's second swing, I was flying through the air and headed for a hard landing. Those who rushed to me the second I hit the ground found I had neither pulse nor breath. My body turned blue; I was clearly dead. But Jerin shouted for someone to phone 911 and knelt to administer cardiopulmonary and mouth-to-mouth resuscitation. My mother, too, rushed to my side.

What I remember is being in the throes of a strange dream and telling myself I needed to remember it so I could tell my mother about it later. Then faraway voices came gradually closer until I could make out someone saying, "We love you, Tao. Come back." Shapes slowly took form until I could see a ring of people around me. At first the people's faces seemed bleary and far away; then they grew clearer and closer. That's when I realized I'd been in some kind of accident. Next, my arm and fingers began hurting, sirens sounded, and I could see paramedics running toward me. My first thought was, "I hope I don't need any injections." As a kid, I hated shots.

I was taken to the hospital and released by evening with a cast on my broken arm, but my internal organs were still sufficiently messed up that I could hold down no food until the next day. What I remember most is trying to eat broccoli soup that night for dinner. It was the best broccoli soup I had ever tasted, but after every ten spoonfuls or so, I would go outside and puke. I did this three or four times before I finally gave up on eating. Although I'd been ordered to wear the arm cast for six weeks, I was so sick of wearing it by the third week that I found a pair of scissors and cut it off myself.

In eighth grade, I was still a brawler, and getting into alcohol and pot as well. But by ninth grade I'd dropped experimenting with those. The wrestling kept me sane, but when the coach demanded that we train six days a week, I bailed. As I saw it, weekends were for outdoor sports—end of story.

My mother, still trying to shift my focus away from school fighting, offered to rent an inflatable kayak one weekend when I was fourteen. She figured we could paddle it down a Class III section of the Skykomish

Christian Knight

One weekend, my brother and I drove to Index, Washington, and applied to be raft guide apprentices. When we started to negotiate our salary, Chris—the owner of the company—mentioned an employee named Cody, which was the name Tao was going by at that time. She said, "His balls are bigger than his brains, and you'd better not be like that."

I soon learned that Chris wasn't always happy. She had dropped out of high school and run away from home to live her life the way she wanted. If you weren't confident in your abilities, sometimes she'd dis you. If you did something she considered stupid, she'd say, "You pulled a Cody." It got to me really badly. It never got to Tao.

Tao was a little guy then, fourteen. I was seventeen and just about to graduate from high school. The first thing he said to me was, "You're so lucky you're going to graduate from high school!" He hated school, didn't want to be there.

My first impression, thanks partly to Chris, was that he was not a smart dude, kind of a meathead. I later realized he definitely wasn't stupid. Chris had asked us to move a railroad tie from her property to where the rafts put in, a hundred-yard carry. We had a truck at our disposal, and the logical thing would have been to put the tie in the truck. But Tao wanted to move it by hoisting it on his shoulders, I think because there were some customers over the way and he had his shirt off.

Very early on, Tao took a distinct interest in me as a paddler. He taught me how to roll. He was there when I first ran Boulder Drop, a Class IV rapid on the Skykomish River. He egged me on to do it.

Tao was a notch above us because it was his second or third season with Chris. He'd prepare salads and marinate the chicken, and on weekends cook it for the customers after safety kayaking. That was fairly glamorous compared with what I had to do: pull weeds and spray for ants on Chris's property. When Tao and I became friends, we were always getting into trouble there.

Our first few years of paddling together formed our relationship and gave me the essence of Tao. He always wanted to push things hard, to see what he couldn't do. I wasn't a very good kayaker, now that I look back on it. So we were commonly getting into these pretty scary situations, which bonded us. He was a big influence on me, definitely pushing it and pushing us. He was pretty crazy. I didn't know how he was going to survive.

River. I happily agreed. But as we were about to put in, we saw a sign indicating that helmets were required. Mom sighed, drove to the nearest rafting outfitter, and asked if we could borrow helmets.

I spent much of the trip trying to paddle us toward the rough-water portions of the river while Mom kept trying to pull us in the opposite direction. That meant we did a lot of the river sideways. Also, because Mom was seated behind me and neither of us had any idea what we were doing, Mom's paddle kept hitting me on the head by accident. Still, as the sun baked down and the cool water splashed in, we grinned and enjoyed the exercise.

Several hours later, we were back in the shop returning the helmets. Mom struck up a conversation with the young woman behind the counter. I was so pumped from the fun ride that I was probably half bouncing off the walls with stories of our fearless exploits. Chris, the owner, was sufficiently bemused that she offered to let me tag along on a trip scheduled for the following weekend on the Nahatlatch, a Class IV river several hundred miles north in British Columbia. Mom's reaction was, "Go for it." That's one great thing about my mom. She was never one to stop us from going on adventures—not until I got into hard-core kayaking and she started fearing for my life. But that's another story.

Chris and her boyfriend, Paul, didn't charge me for that trip, and if they worked me superhard, I certainly didn't notice. All I know is that I fell in love with whitewater that weekend, and they seemed impressed by my enthusiasm and strength. As we relaxed around the campfire on Saturday evening, Chris joked, "I'm going to make you into a world-class kayaker." Paul chuckled and declared, "No, I'm going to make you into a world-class climber." My fourteen-year-old face glowed in the firelight as I thought, *Both sound good to me.*

It was a turning point in my life in so many ways. First, Chris and Paul hired me as a weekend worker, thereby limiting my exposure to the Monroe scenes that were getting me into trouble. Legally, I couldn't guide rafts until I was eighteen, but there was plenty of work making meals for clients, mending rafts, and doing whatever other Joe-jobs occurred to Chris. Secondly, both she and Paul made good on their promises to teach me these new sports, and I was as keen a student as they come. Chris could be moody, and as an employer she was very demanding, but I let any negativity roll right off me. I was used to hard work, and being on rivers made me happier than I'd ever been, if only because it got me away from the school social scene. I owe so much to Chris. If not for her, I'd probably never have gotten into kayaking. She created the opportunity for me, and I will never forget how much she helped me through my early years of paddling.

I ended up working for her for several years, quickly graduating to kayak support, which meant I got to paddle my kayak alongside the rafts, ready to retrieve paddles or customers who got bounced out into the waves.

One weekend, when Chris broke her paddle and had to bail out of a Class V series of whitewater rapids, I decided to finish the challenging rapids alone. The high of that success led me to ever more hard-core paddling. Looking back, I realize that Chris gave me and kids like me opportunities we'd never have had otherwise. That is how I choose to remember her.

Also, that job led me to hang out with much older people, something that perhaps came naturally to a kid like me. After all, I'd learned to walk home alone in the darkness of a bear-ridden mountaintop at the age of seven, and I'd been given more responsibilities and independence than most kids twice my age all through my life. And the more I hung out with the older guides, the more my other life—fighting and drinking—looked incredibly immature. So I stopped, just like that. Although some of the kids in my new older group smoked pot, I didn't get into it. Besides, I was hanging with them during the day, not at night, so my exposure to anything inappropriate was minimal.

Around then, my school introduced a program that allowed me to accelerate my course work, which in turn let me set my sights on finishing my last year of high school at a community college.

That same summer, I fell into my first serious relationship with a girl. Her name was Robin, and we were so crazy about each other that we ended up dating for a year and a half. At first her parents seemed to like me; I was certainly polite and respectful toward them. But they were very strict and religious, in stark contrast to how I'd been raised. As Robin and I got more serious, her mother went from approving to uneasy to freaked out. She became convinced that I was working for the devil to steal her daughter from her. Once, she handed me a Bible and said, "I bet God wouldn't let you read a word out of this." I was pretty dumbfounded. How can you respond to a challenge like that? I don't have a problem with Christians at all, but Robin's family was really hard to deal with.

Determined to pull us apart, Robin's mother began telling her husband lies to turn him against me. He actually visited the police and had a restraining order put on me! When that didn't work, he grounded Robin for the entire summer to prevent her from seeing me. When I heard about this, I went to her house, knocked on the door, and asked to speak with her father. I said, "Hey, if I promise never to see your daughter again, will you unground her?"

He agreed, and I never dated her another day in my life. I was pretty cut up—it was a year before I showed an interest in girls again—but I figure we all have difficult times, and those are the times that really define who we are. We can use them to grow, or to wilt.

I did see Robin once after that, years later, when I was kayaking down the Wenatchee River and she was on a raft. I paddled over and said hi, but for me, it was all long over by then. Once I've made a decision, I stick with it. Besides, I'd already determined that the relationship would never have lasted forever and that having a girlfriend could only get in the way of all I wanted to accomplish.

When I turned fifteen, I landed a winter job working at a ski area that allowed me to save up enough to buy a used Honda Civic. Of course, with five months to go before I could get my driver's license, that $2,400 purchase sat in our yard looking terribly sad. The minute I could legally stick the key in the ignition, I drove like a crazy man, racking up as many close calls as an Indy racer over the next year. I remember once taking a thirty-miles-per-hour curve at seventy, which sent me sliding off the road. The car shaved down an entire dirt bank before it stopped.

Even back then, I had no concept of fear or friction. Another time, with Osho in the passenger seat, I took a corner so fast that the car lifted up and flew between two trees. That got me thinking, "I could've killed my brother." I started to understand the physics of what it took to keep a car on the road. I'm lucky my first car wasn't any faster, or I'd probably have killed myself.

Meanwhile, I'd discovered a way to earn more money than an hourly job could offer. I'd read car ads in the paper each morning, searching for deals that might offer a good profit margin. I developed a bit of expertise on Toyota trucks, which at the time were selling in the Seattle area for a thousand dollars more than their listed blue-book price. Knowing that timing is everything, I'd be up early in the morning to make sure I was the first to phone and visit the sellers. I'd buy right on the spot if it looked good. Then I'd flip my purchase by placing an ad in the same paper the next day. During my high school years, I bought and sold maybe eight vehicles, carefully stowing away the profits for whatever grand adventure I might cook up.

Mom was starting to get nervous around then about the type of whitewater I was kayaking. A registered massage therapist by then, she used to tell Paul (Chris's boyfriend), "Hey, if you keep an eye on him, I'll give you free massages."

Well, one day Paul and I and a bunch of kayakers came to a drop that people usually carried their kayaks around. As Paul shouldered his kayak, I took advantage of his back being turned and went for it—with no safety boaters or other precautions in place. I made it through the rapid fine, but when we got back to town, Paul marched up to my mother and said, "Deal's off. I can't control the guy."

Not long after that I decided to paddle Skykomish Falls, a drop that hadn't been run in five years, ever since someone had drowned trying to negotiate it. Following that fatality, paddlers seemed to assume it wasn't navigable, but imagine how little would be accomplished in life if no one ever attempted supposedly "impossible" feats. It didn't look that hard to me as I stood beside it, scouting. Wouldn't you know my mom would be driving by just then. She pulled over and shouted at me across the river. "Tao Berman, don't even think about it!"

"It's okay, Mom. I'll be fine." I was sixteen, old enough to think for myself, I figured.

"Fine," she said icily. "You run that, and I won't pay your car insurance ever again."

Mom

When Tao was fifteen years old, his friend Luke phoned him challenging him to a fight, because he'd seen Tao talking to Robin—Tao's ex-girlfriend, whom Luke was now seeing. I remember Tao sitting and talking on the phone to Luke for forty-five minutes to calm him down. He was saying things like, "Hey, Luke, I thought we were buddies, and I know she's your girlfriend." He talked him out of fighting. What struck me is how clear it was that he really liked Luke. I just remember thinking, well, that's pretty unusual for a fifteen-year-old, to have that kind of patience and maturity and persistence. Sadly, Luke died in a car accident shortly after.

I shrugged, not believing her. I ran the falls successfully—and sure enough, she never paid my car insurance again. Overall, I was a good kid, pretty respectful of her. But she just seemed to be freaking out way too much around then, it seemed to me. Like when I phoned her after the back tire of my BMX bike clipped a fence I was trying to clear. The tire kicked high, throwing me through the air and onto my arm, which broke.

"Mom, can you take me to the hospital?" I asked politely.

"Tao Berman, I just filled our entire car with groceries, and you're going to help me empty them into the fridge before I take you anywhere."

Fair enough. I biked one-armed across town, cradling the injured one. I helped her unload perishables, then got my ride to the hospital.

I was still fifteen and working summers for Chris when she hired a clean-cut. eighteen-year-old raft guide named Christian Knight. I liked Christian straightaway, and despite the age difference, we soon found that our mutual interest in whitewater kayaking bonded us tightly. I had about nine months' kayaking experience on Christian. Together, we started kayaking harder and harder rapids during our off-hours. Although Christian was a more conservative paddler than I was, he had this notion that taking risks would escalate his skill level. So he'd do things like paddle close to a logjam on purpose. Once, he got sucked under one. Although fate let him out the other side that day, he realized how easily he could have drowned. Even so, nothing slowed us down. In our minds, we were immortal. Either that, or we just didn't care about the consequences. At least, that's the way I saw it. Christian would find a dangerous Cascades creek that had never been run, and he'd challenge me: "Found one I bet you can't do." Looking back, I find it amazing that we lived through that time in our lives. I actually remember one month in which I watched six friends almost drown.

So for months we ran around the Cascades looking for hairy whitewater and living the adage "That which doesn't kill you makes you a better paddler." I think we did a decent job of assessing how far we could push things without killing ourselves. But we were also just really lucky. Because we didn't know any seasoned paddlers willing to paddle what we were paddling, we had no one telling us what we couldn't do, which really influenced us to push things. I frequently wonder how often people don't reach their full potential because someone says what they're trying to accomplish can't be done. I hate the word *can't* and regard anything someone says is impossible as a challenge. Nothing is impossible, just improbable. Anyway, Christian and I felt we had to do the hard sections on our own, and we were having a good time.

One January, Christian, his brother Josh, and I were feeling desperate to paddle. In wintertime, rivers are typically too low to offer much choice. So we drove to Leavenworth, Washington, to paddle Tumwater Canyon, a Class V even when the thermometer isn't hovering at seven degrees Fahrenheit. We stood on the icy riverbank, our breaths steaming the frigid air.

"Cold here," Josh commented, shivering.

"Ice on the edge of the river," I observed.

"Mmmm, we can pull our kayaks up to the snowbank and seal-launch," Christian enthused.

Perfect. We donned helmets, dry-suit tops, and wet suits and tugged our boats to the top of the snowy bank. We snapped our spray decks into place. (Spray decks are neoprene skirts that are elasticized to create a seal at both the paddler's waist and the boat cockpit combing. They're designed to keep water out of the boat, but they can be yanked off if the paddler capsizes, fails to roll up, and needs to swim out of his upside-down boat.) Finally, we jabbed our paddles into the snow to kick off. We slid down the bank like playful seals, our boats skidding across the river's left-hand ice shelf until our bows sliced through its thinnest crust. As we bobbed to the surface of the dark, steaming ribbon of water, we pointed our boats downstream and shouted something like "Yes!" into the still winter air. Already, our boats were covered in a quarter inch of ice.

The first rapid was a quarter mile long. We knew that if we flipped over, chances were strong that our upside-down boats would slide under the ice before we had a chance to roll up. This would be fatal; the ice would act like an undercut rock, one of the more serious obstacles a kayaker can encounter. Josh, as it turned out, did go over and "wet exit" (pull his spray deck's grab loop and swim out of his boat). But somehow, he managed to end up in a pool below the rapid.

At the end of the first rapid, everything but our skin was covered in a layer of ice. In fact, our dry suits were literally frozen onto us. So we drove to the nearest McDonald's and hung out in the men's bathroom, laughing and shivering until we could unzip our gear and change into warm, dry clothing.

That spring, as hard rains put many rivers into flood conditions, a bunch of paddling friends and I decided to attempt a run down the Robe Canyon near Granite Falls, Washington. However, the night before we drove there, it had rained so hard that the river had grown huge. People normally paddled it when its scale read between five and six feet; it was

Christian Knight

Once, I was hitchhiking home from community college when Tao pulled over. As I hopped in, he said, "Watch this. I'm about to make money from a car dealer." We stopped at a dealership, and he proceeded to convince this used-car dealer to buy his used car. In other words, he conned a con man. He didn't sell him a lemon; he just sold him the vehicle for more than he bought it for.

now over the ten-foot mark. Put that much water through a narrow canyon, and there's nowhere for it to go but straight up. That's when river hydraulics do very strange things. Massive plumes of water shoot high into the air, and eddy edges known as "fences" form boils, which are pretty much like whirlpools.

Normally, kayakers navigate rivers by weaving from one eddy to another. In other words, they literally "eddy hop" their way down a river. Typically, eddies are miniharbors: calm little pools of counterflow along river edges and just below large boulders. They allow a period of rest as well as an opportunity to scout an upcoming rapid without climbing out of one's boat. Eddies, then, are normally a kayaker's best friend and generally more or less level with the downstream current beside them. That means they're usually pretty easy to cruise into.

When eddies grow "fences" at high water, on the other hand, this complicates a kayaker's life. Fences mean the swirling eddy is perhaps a few inches above the rest of the river. This forces the paddler to aim his bow at just the right angle and speed in order to pierce the "fence" and climb atop the eddy for that all-important rest and reconnaissance. It takes a skilled paddler to negotiate even small eddy fences without capsizing, and an equally skilled paddler to roll up after capsizing in eddy-fence conditions. But the alternative to catching eddies—with fences or without—is to run the river "blind," without the pauses so crucial for checking out what's immediately ahead and figuring out how to tackle it.

Rivers with eddy fences several feet high are diabolical. There, the currents are so angry that a paddler who fails to roll and ejects from his boat is more than likely to drown. This I knew as my eight friends and I emerged from the car and stared wide-eyed at the Stillaguamish River.

If I swim, I reflected, it will be a complete miracle if I survive. And once I paddle into the canyon, there's no way to get to shore and walk out. The walls tower straight up, committing you from start to finish. (For some reason, I've always been able to calculate the odds of my survival with complete detachment.) I was sixteen and into testing myself. No one had ever run Robe Canyon this high, which is why the guys standing around me made a sensible decision. "No way," they ruled. "Let's go do another river."

"Okay, but just drop me off at the top and come back to pick me up when you've finished the other river," I requested.

At first they refused, but I basically pleaded with them until they agreed. As they drove away and I entered the flow of the river, I started to get excited. On the very first rapid, jets of water were exploding twenty to twenty-five feet into the air. I shot between them like a pinball, reflecting on the fact that if a wave were to blow my spray deck off, I'd be dead meat. The eddy lines were monstrous: three to four feet high. Just getting into and out of eddies was a major chore. Never had I felt so small and vulnerable; I was like a gnat in a draining bathtub. My boat tore down that river at a blurring speed. I rolled a few times, thankful each time I came up. In half the time it normally takes to paddle the river, I was at the takeout. Alive, and alone.

I waited for my buddies. I waited and waited. I knew there was a pay phone a mile away. To get a ride home, all I had to do was walk there and phone my mom. But then she'd know what I'd done, and I'd be hung out to dry, so to speak. So I waited all the way until dusk, lying full length on my bright-orange overturned boat. Above me, treetops waved and birds soared against a darkening sky. Beside me, shadows lengthened until only the foamy wave tips of the roaring rapids glinted in the twilight.

Finally, I gave up. I walked the mile to use the pay phone and
made the call home. Of course, as I reluctantly explained my predicament
to my distressed mom, wouldn't you know the guys pulled up to get me?
So I got my ride home and got in trouble for doing the first solo descent of
the Robe.

At sixteen, I may have tamed my tendency to raise my fists whenever someone challenged me, but my enthusiasm for testing myself had
only just begun. In a sense, I just transferred my fighting mentality to
this new scene, to pushing the limits of what I could do in my kayak.
I still couldn't back away from a challenge, but now the challenge was
whitewater, where the risks were greater than a black eye. Long since, I've
accepted that this is a part of me I can't change. Back then, though, whitewater was just one facet of that burning need I had to explore my own
physical limits. When my dentist ordered me to have four wisdom teeth
taken out that year, I set myself the goal of taking no painkillers. My
face swelled up such that I barely recognized myself, and for two nights
I couldn't sleep, but my stubbornness held. No pain pill passed my lips
throughout the ordeal.

Then there was rock climbing. When I decided I wanted to climb
a seven hundred-foot vertical rock wall near where we lived, I called my
friend Josh (Christian's brother), who agreed to join me in my quest. Both
of us were pushing our skill levels, big-time. The route up was difficult by
any standards. When at last we wiped the sweat from our foreheads and
enjoyed our eagle's-eye view, it was time to rappel down.

"I'm going down to the first ledge," Josh announced as he unwound
a length of rope and attached a belay device to it. "Then it'll be your turn."

"Sounds good," I agreed.

Unfortunately, Josh lowered himself fifty feet past the ledge before he realized his mistake. He was now dangling six hundred feet in the air at the end of his rope.

"Pull yourself up the rope with one arm," I shouted through cupped hands, trying to hold back a chuckle at his error. "Then take some slack out of the belay device and do it again!" I was rocking back and forth precariously on the top of the wall, belly laughing at his predicament. I know this was an inappropriate response, but back then, it's how I always dealt with sketchy situations. Back then, my friends and I got into so many such situations that we turned them into jokes.

He looked up and sneered, not appreciating my sense of humor. But my instructions were his only option. Eventually, of course, he managed to muscle his way up the equivalent of five stories. Otherwise we'd have had a big problem; we didn't know enough back then to set up prusiks or use ascenders.

Also at age sixteen, I read a book about soldiers sleeping in the muddy trenches of World War I. Curious as to how lousy their experience really was and how I'd have fared, I scouted out a little ditch near our house and waited for a rainy night. When it arrived, I climbed out the window with my sleeping bag and curled up in my make-believe trench. Of course, the water accumulated quickly, soaking my bag and reducing me to shivers as I tried to flex my muscles to stay warm. I coaxed my black Labrador retriever into my bag once, but she soon escaped and hid under the car, not to be coaxed out. I lay in that puddle until daylight, then rose and went whitewater kayaking, having proved—well, I suppose having proved—that I was a silly sixteen-year-old.

chapter four

LIFE AT THE EDGE

"It has to be real enough to kill you."

—Willi Unsoeld,
American mountaineer

t was late summer, the sun high and hot over the cold, bony creek we were paddling. "Bony" is what kayakers call creeks so low on water that normally hidden boulders appear to rise like sunbathing hippos to form an obstacle course. They constrict passageways, grab at paddles, and smack boats attempting to slither past.

Four of us were working our way down this water-starved Class V stream named the Ohanepecosh: Christian, me, and friends named Tembe and Morgan. Our paddles dipped rhythmically beneath a majestic view of snowcapped Mount Rainier as we slalomed around the overpopulation of rocks, listening for the rumble of upcoming rapids.

I was in the lead when we approached a horizon line emitting a freight-train roar. This meant a drop so steep that we could not scout it without drifting so close that there'd be no turning back. More-cautious boaters would have paddled to shore, climbed out of their kayaks, and hiked to where they could see what was ahead. But we had developed a no-scout ethic, meaning that wherever possible, we would attempt to catch a small eddy right before a big drop and scan what was below without getting out of our boats. This kept us on edge because we knew that if we missed the eddy, we would be swept down the falls without having scouted. The point, of course, was to make a difficult river even more dangerous. We liked to joke, "You can run a drop blind only once."

Being the most experienced paddler in the group, I volunteered to go first, as usual. I sped up and greeted the falls with a sprint that sent me flying over its lip. I landed neatly in the pool below and maneuvered to where the others could see my signal.

Now that I was below the drop, I had a chance to analyze it. The ledge fell only about six feet to the pool beside which I was now sitting.

But a foot past its upper lip, it wore a necklace of wood: a pair of logs that stretched from bank to bank like a gill net. I'd paddled so hard that the logs had served as a nice ramp, propelling the boat far enough out that I had landed beyond the falls' backwash.

But if anyone paddled over the lip with a hint of indecision, those logs could easily thwart his takeoff and shove him back into the waterfall.

I knew Morgan was planning to go next. He was the least skilled but gutsiest of the three now waiting for my signal. I motioned for him to pour on as much speed as possible, and I raised my thumb in the late afternoon's waning light.

As soon as Morgan glimpsed my thumbs-up, he was off. The nose of his boat dropped complacently over the lip. He slid over the first log and out onto the second. I thought he was clear. But just before he would have joined me in the pool, his forward momentum vanished. Gravity yanked him backward and twisted him like a dog on a leash. He was now sideways to the falls like a silhouette, his tail wedged between the ledge and logs and his bow pointing to the sky.

My jaw loosened, and for a few moments, I couldn't think of a solution. On his upstream side was the ledge, pulsing water over its lip. Some of the splashes washed Morgan's tense face. Slowly but surely, that falling water was squeezing the bottom of his boat onto the log.

He was calm at first because in this position, he could still breathe. Quickly, I waved Christian and Tembe to beach their boats and scramble down to help me. All four of us had been through swift-water rescue training, but never had we seen or heard of a situation like this. Most vertical pins involve the bow, not the stern. And most of the time, just the tip of the bow is lodged under a rock, under water. In such cases, the

rescue—while frantic and dicey—is simple: either dislodge the boat by yanking it upstream with ropes and carabiners, or dislodge the boater by yanking him upstream with rescue ropes. But neither of those techniques was applicable to Morgan's case.

The upper log was imprisoning him not by the tip of his bow, but by the cockpit area of his kayak. To have adapted the standard plan to Morgan's situation, the three of us would have had to have lifted him and his boat into the air, using our combined strength and the platform of an algae-slimed twelve-inch log—all while struggling against the force of the water and the weight of Morgan (one hundred ninety pounds) and his kayak (forty pounds). The notion was so unconvincing that none of us even bothered to mention it.

As we racked our brains for other rescue ideas, Morgan's delicate position was deteriorating. His boat was sinking bit by bit, wrapping itself ever so slightly onto the log. This, in turn, was thrusting his head more directly into the waterfall. If he stared into the sky, the waterfall would dump squarely onto his face. So, just to grab breaths of air, Morgan was forced to turn his head from side to side, like a toddler screaming "no."

To buy time, I positioned myself on the river's left bank and asked Tembe and Christian to throw me one end of a rescue rope from where they stood on the right bank. Christian did so, keeping hold of the other end so that we now had a line across the pool. Together, Christian and I slid that rope behind Morgan's back—between him and the ledge—and tightened it to help hold him away from the curtain of water. It also made it easier for him to lean forward against his bow to create an air pocket for breathing, even as he sat in his near-vertical boat. For now, at least, he was able to breathe more easily.

But we knew that the solution was temporary, effective for a few minutes at the most, because the lower part of his boat was still slowly flattening itself against the log. In fact, the torrent of water falling between the ledge and Morgan had swallowed Morgan's stern at this point.

Morgan, who'd dropped his paddle, motioned toward where the boat was beginning to exert pressure against his legs. Clearly, the boat was wrapping on the log. I knew that if the boat broke and wrapped more completely, it would be nearly impossible to help him.

I checked the throw rope that was holding Morgan's torso against the bow of his boat and noted that, already, his air pocket was vanishing.

"Help me!" Morgan said, his voice now desperate and garbled by the water pushing into his mouth. "Whatever you're going to do, do it quickly!"

I knew we couldn't pull him out of his boat, and I knew we couldn't pull his boat out. I also knew his air pocket would be completely gone in about two minutes. At that point, we'd have five minutes to get him out before he drowned. The only solution I could think of was potentially fatal. Together, the three of us might be able to push Morgan downward—between the logs and into the aerated pool, under water. If we were strong enough, and if the river was deep enough, his boat would disappear under the logs and resurface downstream.

If our thrust wasn't powerful enough or, more importantly, if the river wasn't deep enough, his stern would pin on the bottom of the river. There, submerged, he'd have no hope of air, and we'd have no hope of reaching down and lifting him back up. He'd be dead in the span of a television show's commercial break.

Christian Knight

Very early on in our relationship, I told Tao that some friends and I were on our way to the North Fork of the Skykomish to raft it. He told me not to do it, that the idea was stupid, that we'd get our raft wrapped around a rock. We said we were doing it regardless, so he drove us up there. He was sixteen and had this red Honda, and he was driving really fast up a road with hairpin turns and blind hills. And all the time he was playing Bryan Adams, which no respectable teenager had played for six years. I realized he was disconnected from pop culture; he didn't even know who Tom Cruise was.

I looked over at Morgan. He was thrashing his head back and forth, searching for a breath of air. We had no choice. I relayed the plan to Christian and Tembe. Tembe agreed, but Christian was reluctant.

"What if the river's not deep enough?" he screamed over the roar of the falls. "He'll die."

"Christian!" I said. "We have no other choice!"

Christian looked around as if searching for another solution. He stared at the throw ropes, the logs, and the waterfall. He shook his head.

"Okay," he said, eyes avoiding mine. "Let's do it quickly."

All three of us positioned ourselves on the log entrapping Morgan's boat. Together, we placed our hands on his bow. Morgan was barely able to breathe at this point, and he couldn't hear. But he figured out what we were about to do, and he held up his thumb.

"On the count of three," I said. "One. Two. Three."

Three strong guys working together make for a pretty powerful force. Morgan's boat responded. It slithered downward into the pool, releasing itself from the log, until the white, bubbly water swallowed its last tip.

Morgan and his boat had both vanished. We swiveled our heads downstream and waited with dry throats. It couldn't have been more than seconds, but it seemed a lot longer. At last, Morgan's boat surfaced, upside down. The boat jiggled the way boats do when someone is performing a wet exit from beneath them. Then Morgan's helmeted head popped up. He was gasping. He was alive.

Christian looked at me long and hard, and said, "It worked out. You think fast, and you act fast."

I was seventeen, and Christian and I had been kayaking together for three years by then. He'd become my best friend, which he remains to this day. On this particular trip, Christian managed to get two snapshots of me coming over various falls. I was pleased about that as the two of us drove home later—so pleased that I impulsively pulled over where the road passed Werner Paddles in Sultan, Washington.

"I'm going to see if I can get them to sponsor me," I announced, cutting the car's engine and holding up the snapshots with a grin. I was both broke and in need of a paddle at the time.

Christian shook his head and rolled his eyes at my nerve, clearly thinking I was unbelievably full of myself and wasting my time. Ten minutes later, I emerged grinning, pumping my hand in the air and saying "Yes!"

There are companies that hand out sponsorships relatively easily, but Werner has never been one of them. I wasn't much known at the time; at that point, I figure, Christian could just as easily have secured sponsorship. But I was the one with the guts to walk in there with two out-of-focus snapshots, brazenly asking for my first sponsorship.

Christian shook his head in disbelief. "You're pulling my leg, Cody, right?"

"Nope. By the way, I'm Tao again," I announced. I'd been considering changing my name back for a while, but this clinched the decision. If I was going after sponsorships, "Tao" was a far more memorable name than "Cody." Maybe my parents had done me a favor after all.

"Whatever," Christian replied, grinning with a mixture of disbelief, jealousy, and pride.

At that point, Christian was twenty and studying journalism at a community college. And I'd jumped a year ahead in high school by signing up for an alternative program that had me getting high school credits for courses at a different community college. My favorite class, of course, was PE, but I managed As and Bs in the others. I always put in just enough work to get good grades.

With high school graduation looming (I never attended the ceremony because I wasn't going back to that school more than I had to), I knew I couldn't keep living at my mom's. I needed a way to earn money, and I needed a plan. In the short term, my goal was to run the absolute hardest water I physically could without killing myself. I had two thousand dollars saved up and two buddies (Brett Kerrin and Gavin

Dad

I tried to consciously engage both Tao and
Osho to think for themselves and develop
their own worldview.

McClurg) with whom we had cooked up the idea of heading to Mexico
and Central America and paddling there until our money ran out. After
that, maybe I'd enter college and study marketing. The notion of paddling
for a living hadn't yet taken root, although the Werner sponsorship had
definitely whetted my appetite.

So, in August of 1997, the three of us loaded Gavin's nineteen-foot
Chevy van with boats and boating gear. I also threw in a little Hi8 video
camera, hoping to capture exciting footage to bring back to my friends.
We rolled out of Index, Washington, and drove two thousand miles to
Baja California.

We spent three weeks in Baja, some of the most miserable weeks of
my life. Recently hit by the weather phenomenon El Niño, the region and
its ocean water were so unbearably hot that dead fish were washing up on
the beaches. It was too hot to sleep, even at night. I remember lying naked
under the stars, sweating profusely.

Late one afternoon, bored out of our minds, we noticed an island
barely visible from shore and got into a debate as to how far away it was.

Gavin guessed it was fifty miles and bet me one hundred dollars I couldn't paddle there and back. That's all it took for me to launch from our beach campsite and paddle my short boat against gusty winds. I counted my strokes by the thousand for something to do and was pretty pleased to arrive about four hours later while it was still barely light. Of course, the "island" turned out to be an uninhabitable rock, so after eating the avocado I'd brought along as a snack and stuffing a rock into my pocket to prove I'd made it, I made the rash decision to paddle back to my camp mates. It was either that or spend all night on the island. Unfortunately, the winds had shifted, forcing me to paddle against both the wind and tide. As it grew dark, I refused to worry. I was pretty sure I knew where to head. I suffered a short bout of nervousness when I saw the lights of a huge ship bearing down on me. There's no way the ship's navigators could see me, so I went into a sprint to get out of its way, thinking, "I made a stupid bet for a hundred dollars, and now I'm going to get run over by a ship for it?"

Happily, the ship passed without hitting me, but by then I realized the tide was pushing me farther out into the ocean. I was at least a couple of miles off course. I could see where the guys were flashing the van's headlights to guide me in, and I tried to head toward them. But just as I thought I might be getting close, something hit me hard. It was a wave, I realized as I squinted into the dark—a wave bouncing off rocky cliffs directly in front of me.

I did my best to surf in toward the cliff walls without getting smashed against them. Paddling sideways down each wave, I managed not to capsize—just as well, as I was wearing neither life jacket nor helmet. Then I had to power back out through the waves before paddling toward camp, now several miles away along the shore. Every ten minutes,

I'd see my friends' lights flash. They were pretty relieved to see me when I beached around midnight, finishing a seven- to eight-hour paddle. Of course, I'd done it for the adventure, and I felt bad about taking my buddy's money, so I told him just to buy me tacos the next day.

The three of us had arranged for girlfriends to fly down and meet us in Baja at one point. But we didn't exactly enjoy romantic interludes. Instead, our relationships all fried in the heat. We were pretty relieved to see the girls off at Cabo Airport just before we boarded the ferry for mainland Mexico.

We'd brought with us an *American Whitewater* magazine article about some guys who'd paddled whitewater in Mexico. The authors hadn't included directions, but we used that article like a treasure map, continually cross-referencing it with our map of Mexico to guess where they'd paddled. The article mentioned finishing a run at "an unrunnable, 100-foot-plus cascading waterfall."

Well, ever since I discovered kayaking, I've had this thing about the word *unrunnable*. I just had to find this waterfall and try to prove them wrong. Once I'd figured out it was on the El Salto River, that's where we headed, paddling some pretty crazy stuff along the way. It was a wild trip—so hot that there seemed nothing to do but drink. Brett was always the instigator when it came to alcohol. He would walk out of Mexican markets with a case of Corona and a big grin. I've never been a big drinker, but this trip was an exception. Also, being eighteen and in a different country that had long, straight roads and few other drivers, we often drove like there were no laws. En route to El Salto, we kept getting stopped by policemen asking for bribes in exchange for letting us carry on. I knew absolutely no Spanish, but Gavin was pretty good with the language. Each time the police asked, we said, "Sorry, we haven't got any money. Go ahead and put us in jail if you have to." They let us alone every time.

When we finally reached El Salto, we had a fun time running the clear, turquoise river down to the falls. It was a playful but not intimidating river: a few Class V rapids, including a twenty-five-foot waterfall. The sun baked the lush green jungle. There were no villages or people along the way, but by the time we reached the "unrunnable" falls, and I scouted it and decided to go for it, a dozen locals had gathered to watch. They may or may not have seen kayakers before, but they sure hadn't seen any paddlers going for something like this.

Osho

Tao made a very deliberate decision in high school to stop partying and focus on kayaking. From there on, he kind of left people his own age behind. He took a lot of criticism for it, but he was undeterred. I didn't understand why he'd walk away from hanging out with people considered cool. But he and Lilly both had a lot of older friends.

The waterfall itself was both powerful and pretty. Aqua blue against travertine rock, it squeezed the entire river over its lip before letting the water drop about one hundred thirty-five feet in three tiers. There was a twenty-foot drop into a pool no longer than a kayak's length, then a thirty-five-foot drop into an equally stingy and shallow pool, and finally an eighty-foot plunge before El Salto picked itself up and ambled on. I reminded myself that it was crucial to hit each pool with my bow slightly up so that the boat would land flat rather than "piton" (fall like an arrow attempting to pierce the pool's underwater rocks). The worst-case scenario would be capsizing in one of the pools, which weren't long enough to allow a recovery. Given the rough rock lurking beneath those curtains of falling water, the last thing I wanted was to go over that final eighty-foot drop upside down. It would either give me a nasty face job or knock me unconscious.

I gazed down to where Brett was positioned with a rescue rope and Gavin was holding my video camera. I sprinted toward the first lip and enthralled the cheering villagers by nailing my intended line; it was a perfect run. I was so psyched that, despite a hard rainfall that night, I decided to run it again the next day.

The sun had replaced the black clouds by the time I positioned myself at the top again. I noticed that the crowd had swelled as much as the river. I paddled hard toward the roaring water and thrilled to the sensation of going airborne once again. I splashed neatly into the first pool and soared over the second tier. But as my boat entered the second pool, my bow struck rock, so hard that it felt like someone had punched me in the gut. My boat started to swivel, as if determined to dump me in headfirst. I couldn't allow this to happen, so as the kayak began to spin, I did a quick move that converted the momentum into a full cartwheel. The boat fell forward, stern-over-bow-over-stern. I ended up backward but right side up as I went over the final lip.

This is not the type of situation that allows you to call a time-out and formulate a plan; it demands a reaction driven purely by trained instincts and balance. Maybe I was born with some of that, maybe I developed it during an active childhood, maybe I'd honed it with all the crazy paddling I'd been doing since age fourteen. I have no idea. I just know that time after time, instinct and balance have served me well, have saved my skin. Certainly, they helped counter the daredevilry mixed with adolescent foolishness that was in full bloom on this trip. In any case, under the circumstances of that run, the cartwheel was definitely the best bet. I landed in the final pool with no further mishap. My buddies looked relieved. Neither of them volunteered to run the falls themselves. I named that falls "Welcome to Insanity."

The same name would have been appropriate for an adventure the three of us had on the Rio Santa Maria. We'd heard that the Rio Santa Maria was good, and we figured out where the put-in was. We had no idea where the takeout was; we never even studied the map to check whether the bends in the river might come near a road again. We had this adolescent need to wing it, a need to experience adventure to the fullest. This trip was definitely not about being safe.

So we just parked Gavin's van and started stuffing gear into our boats. Figuring it would be a two-day paddle, Brett and I stowed tarps, energy bars, and lots of water bottles in our kayaks. When I saw Gavin pushing a hammock into his, I said, "Gavin, what if it rains? Sure you don't want to take a tarp?"

"Nah, I'll be fine," he replied.

The first day's paddle was pleasant enough. We played so hard that we were happy to pull off at dusk for a night's shut-eye. The next day, the river entered a narrow canyon, which wound along until we found ourselves at the foot of a three hundred-foot waterfall pouring in over our canyon's left-side wall. Whoa, what a waterfall. Like a fire hose pouring full volume into a trickle of water, it all but engulfed the river we were paddling, for a full rapid's length. There was no way we could power into those roiling hydraulics without killing ourselves, so we had to portage around the turbulence.

The canyon walls that bound our river rose steeply on both our left and right sides. That left us two options. The first was to scramble up the wall on our right, then hike along its rim until we were downstream of the waterfall-fed rapid, at which point we could lower ourselves and our boats back to the river. The second, more dubious option was to climb the wall on out left beside the roaring waterfall, then somehow fjord or paddle across the unseen stream forming the waterfall, and finally hike along the left-hand rim of the canyon's wall to where we could lower ourselves back to our river. Since we had no visual on the stream that was feeding the falls, we went for the less risky option of climbing out of the canyon on the right side. We had no climbing ropes, only our eighty-foot rescue ropes.

I was the best climber, so I started making like Spider-Man up the slimy, vertical wall. As soon I reached something like eighty feet, I

Grandma Doreen

Tao was always a very positive child, eager to enter into whatever was on tap, full-heartedly. But like his father, he's also reflective and socially appealing, someone people take to.

positioned myself on a ledge big enough to hold the boats and threw the ropes down. The guys tied the kayaks on, and I pulled them up one by one. Then the guys free-climbed up to join me, after which we repeated the process higher up. Once up on the canyon rim, we could see across to the stream feeding the falls. I shook my head in frustration. Only now could we see that it would have been a dead-simple ferry across that upper stream in our kayaks: no significant obstacles for a long way upstream of the falls, no chance of getting swept over the falls. And the wall beside the falls would have made for much easier climbing than the one we'd just sweated our way up.

"No way," I said glumly.

"Figures," Gavin said.

"Should've taken our changes climbing up the other side. Would've been way, way less trouble," Brett declared.

Of course, it was too late by then. There was nothing to do but walk the 200 yards along the rim, past the big river's falls-fed rapid, and then start back down the wall. We'd put in twelve sweaty hours by the time we were back on the river. By then it was dusk and drizzling. We managed to paddle a few miles before darkness dictated that we beach. We tugged our kayaks up into a cow pasture. Unfortunately for our growling stomachs, we'd eaten our last energy bar for lunch. Oh, well, our eyelids were pretty heavy anyway. But hardly had I rolled myself up in my tarp when the sky turned pitch black and the drizzle crescendoed into a downpour of biblical proportions.

My tarp had a few holes in it, and the water soon found them. For hours, I tossed and turned in several inches of water, slowly turning into a prune. Beside me, Gavin was far more miserable, sleeping atop his useless hammock fully exposed to the elements. Nevertheless, I was determined not to invite him in until he asked. Around midnight, I heard his contrite voice.

"Tao, can I share your tarp with you?"

"Of course," I replied, laughing. By then, all three of us had given up trying to sleep, so we spent the rest of the night telling jokes.

"We need food," Brett declared the next morning at first light. The rain had slackened, and we were all shivering.

"Yeah, and I've had enough of paddling this river," Gavin said.

I sat up in my tarp. Streams of water ran down it into the grass. I shook water out of my hair and looked about. I locked eyes with a cow. "Hey, where there are cows, there have to be farmers," Gavin suggested.

We threw our boats onto our shoulders and started slogging through the drenched pasture. When we got to a village alongside a road, Gavin and I left Brett watching our boats and stuck our thumbs out for a ride back to our van. The driver of an old bus stopped and told us he was on his way to a larger town.

"That sounds good," Gavin told him. "We'll hire a taxi from there."

It was luxurious being out of the rain for the fifteen-mile ride to town, despite the bumpy road, the bus's worn shocks, and the smell of unwashed paddlers' bodies. Feeling sorry—but only a little—for Brett, who was still standing in the rain watching our boats, Gavin and I thanked the driver and transferred to a taxi van for another fifteen-mile ride. What we hadn't anticipated was how far the river had risen overnight. The taxi driver frowned as the roads turned muddy. He grimaced when he had to accelerate through water right up to his van's doors. Gavin and I gripped the worn vinyl of the back seat when he powered through a low point that put water right up to the van's hood. But he was a gutsy driver, determined to give us our fare's worth. Even so, he shook his head when he braked in front of our van. It was almost up to its hubs in the swollen river.

"Thanks, dude," Gavin said in Spanish. At least, that's what I assume he said. And we set to the job of backing the van out.

This should be interesting, I thought as Gavin fired it up and swung out and away from the water. Up and down twisty roads we went, sometimes accelerating through water up to our hood. I held my breath once when Gavin gunned it through water up to our windshield. We'd come down here looking for adventure, I reflected as Brett and the pile of kayaks finally came into view, and we sure were getting it.

On one of Gavin's swims, he smashed his leg on a rock and scraped it up badly. Five days later, when the skin surrounding the wound started to grow red, Brett said, "Gavin, that scrape is getting infected."

Gavin studied it with a frown. "You think?"

"Yeah, we gotta open it up and clean it out," Brett insisted.

Gavin narrowed his eyes at Brett, and after a long moment, shrugged. "Okay, do what you think you have to do."

First, Brett grabbed a brush and began scraping the wound, ignoring Gavin's yelling. Then he produced a bottle of tequila.

"Drink lots, then it won't hurt," he said with a hint of a smile.

I shook my head as I held the video camera, but I let the two of them get on with it. It wasn't long before Gavin was pretty wasted. However much Gavin drank, though, Brett's vigorous brushing and scraping was making him yell out. Finally, Brett declared the job done. But a week later, when the wound still displayed red edges without revealing any other signs of infection, we all figured out that the redness was just part of the healing process.

"None of that brushing was necessary!" Gavin accused Brett in a voice thoroughly pissed off.

Brett looked only a little guilty; the rest of us were trying not to laugh aloud.

It was soon after that escapade that Gavin decided he'd had enough and refused to paddle anymore. Essentially, the swims were freaking him out. I sensed that this brought Brett's fear factor into play, too, because now we lacked a third person for safety. Three paddlers is a much safer number if something goes wrong. But I was still into doing the irresponsible thing and wanted to keep pushing it. Although the group dynamics were starting to fall apart, Gavin agreed to serve as our driver for another adventure or two.

"Then I'm going to sell the van and travel through Guatemala on my own," he announced one evening.

I wasn't surprised. Things were becoming strained among the three of us. Anyway, I figured we'd done most of the rivers we'd wanted to do in Mexico. It was time to move on to Guatemala.

"That's cool," I told him. "Brett and I can take buses in Guatemala, even with the kayaks. It'll make things interesting."

"I'd be down with that," Brett agreed. "But you'll shuttle for us on a couple more before you take off, Gavin?"

"I said I would," Gavin replied.

The next morning, Gavin dropped us off at the start of a fifteen-mile river canyon reputed to have some exciting whitewater. Considering how things had gone on the Rio Santa Maria, Brett and I were ridiculously casual about the drop-off. Thinking ahead remained low on our list of priorities. Any fool could've pointed out we'd never be able to do that section in one day. Yet there I was with nothing but a boat, paddle, water bottle, and shortie top—not even a long-sleeved paddling fleece or sleeping bag.

Right away, the canyon showed us who was boss. We were forced to portage our boats about every hundred yards, sometimes climbing up steep canyon walls and rappelling down again short distances farther. At one point we scouted a rapid that ended in a forty-five-foot waterfall that fed most of the water to an undercut rock.

I looked at the steep walls on both sides and saw that not only was there no way to portage around the falls, but there was also no way to climb up and out of the canyon anymore. Also, we'd been warned that the area had lots of drug fields, meaning we'd better stick to the river and

Christian Knight

Tao has humbled out a lot the last three or four years. I've always told him he's arrogant. Even when he was Cody, he was full of himself. Once, he and a friend named Gavin and I were playing on a wave on Tye Creek. Afterwards, Tao was going on and on about how many cartwheels he'd thrown. Gavin started saying the same thing; they had this friendly rivalry going. I said, "You guys are so freaking arrogant I can hardly be in the same car as you." Tao said, "If it's true, how can that be arrogant?" I said, "Just 'cause it's not a lie doesn't mean it's not arrogant."

not make much noise. We sat and contemplated our options as the water thundered over the lip, mocking us.

"There's only one way," Brett suggested. "Throw our kayaks over the falls, then climb along the rocks until we can jump down beyond the undercut, holding our paddles. Then catch our boats and go from there."

I sighed and stared harder at the falls. "You try that," I decided. "I'll take my chances in my kayak."

I went first. My goal was to drop vertically over the falls so that my kayak and I would catch the deep currents likely to take me past the undercut rock before we resurfaced. I was pretty happy when my plan worked. Just beyond the undercut, I eddied out and watched Brett.

First, Brett tossed his kayak over the falls. I secured it as soon as it floated to me. Meanwhile, Brett clambered around rocks high above, clutching his paddle as he attempted to choose a leaping-off place. My head jerked up as I saw his paddle falling before he'd jumped. He hadn't meant to let go. My heart sank as I saw the paddle disappear under the undercut. We waited, and waited some more. The paddle, it seemed, had decided to take up permanent residence under that undercut rock, confirming for us that the currents there were particularly nasty. I heaved a sigh.

Brett and I watched for a long time, waiting for that undercut to spit out his paddle. It never did. So Brett did what he had to do: He leapt from the rocks above into the pool beyond the undercut. He climbed back into his kayak, shot one last rueful glance at where his paddle had disappeared, and started hand-paddling downstream. We were maybe five miles down the fifteen-mile stretch of river. There was nothing for it but for me to peel out and paddle just ahead of Brett, alert for rapids he couldn't hand-paddle. I lifted a whistle from the pocket in my life jacket and stuck it into my mouth so I could warn him of rapids that needed portaging. As I paddled a bend or two ahead of Brett, I reminded myself that we were so deep in this canyon that the whistle's noise couldn't carry up to annoy any drug growers.

We paddled on like this for some time before we came to a drop that, though only a fifteen-footer, featured an undercut eerily like the one that had just stolen Brett's paddle. Except this time, instead of routing itself under a raised rock, the current fed into and out of a small, low-ceilinged cave.

Brett was out of the water and trying to carry around the falls even before I raised the whistle to my lips. *Good,* I thought. Without a paddle, he definitely needs to portage this one. Then I heard a crash and a splash. No way. He'd dropped his boat while attempting to get good footing on the rocks. Naturally, his boat plunged over the falls and followed the current into the cave. There it stayed, whirling around like a newly installed merry-go-round feature.

I didn't need to glance up to know there was no way he could climb out of the canyon.

"I'll paddle into the cave," I offered grimly. "Then you throw me a rope. I'll clip it onto your boat so you can pull it out. Then I'll paddle out."

"Thanks." Brett's voice was hoarse and his eyebrows creased with concern.

I paddled in. He threw the rope. But the rope reached only to the middle of the cave. So I hung onto his boat, waiting for the rotation of the water that would spin us to where I could clip onto the rope. Every time I was about to succeed, the frothy water would slam against me, making me choose between staying upright and finishing the job. I knew if I flipped over, the current could shove me to where the ceiling was so low that I would have difficulty rolling back up. So staying upright was pretty important. For about fifteen minutes, I struggled to leash the kayak, with no luck. Worse, daylight was disappearing on us.

Eventually, the water managed to flip me. I'm sure I cursed silently at that point. I knew that if I came out of my kayak, I'd drown. Without a boat and paddle, I had no hope of powering out of this whirlpool and would be beyond the reach of Brett's rope. Luckily, I managed to roll. And finally, I managed to attach that damn rope.

Brett pulled his boat out, and, with furious paddling, I bade the cave good riddance. So we were out of the cave, but where did that put us? In the darkness of nightfall, which ruled out paddling any farther down river. At this point, we had neither food nor water, and there was nowhere to sleep but a rock ledge beneath the falls, where the mist from the water fell on us all night. We couldn't drink the river water because rivers in Mexico are disgustingly polluted. We got so cold we had to take turns doing jumping jacks and push-ups for eight long hours, getting hungrier and thirstier all the time.

After what seemed an eternity, the sky grew brighter, and we rejoiced that daylight had finally arrived. But we were wrong. It was only the moon rising. Both Brett and I are a bit homophobic, so huddling together for warmth was something we'd consider only as a last resort. But as the night grew colder, we realized we needed all the help we could get to stay warm. So, in between the push-ups and jumping jacks, we lay with our backs touching for whatever heat that would conserve. When daylight dawned, we climbed back into our kayaks and resumed our run: two kayaks, one paddle, and two ravenously hungry, bleary-eyed young men who hadn't slept for more than twenty-four hours.

Before we reached our takeout, however, a ninety-foot waterfall loomed. It was unrunnable even by our standards. Standing over the falls, we tied our kayaks onto our eighty-foot throw rope and lowered them as far as they'd go. Then we dropped the rope to let them fall the final ten feet into the water below. Next, we jumped after them, me first. When Brett jumped, he cried out.

"Tweaked my knee," he admitted, hugging it once we were out of the water.

"Bummer." What more could I say? I watched him limp to his kayak and limp every time he had to get out of it the rest of the day. At this point, all we wanted was to get the hell out of the canyon, but the vertical walls made this impossible. So we kept paddling down river, looking for a way out. The thought of spending another night was really terrible. Happily, we managed to get far enough down the canyon that day that we were able to hike. And walk out we did, kayaks on our shoulders, Brett's injured knee wavering so much that I was afraid he'd topple over any minute. When we came to a hut, Brett greeted the old woman inside it with a plea for agua, meaning water, which the woman was kind enough to give us. A short while later, we stumbled onto a road and bused to town to tell Gavin our tale.

Shortly after that we drove to Guatemala, where Gavin sold his van and Brett and I boarded a bus with our kayaks. It didn't take us long to figure out that this was nothing like going Greyhound in the States. I remember riding one bus whose gas pedal had a bungee cord attached to keep it from falling to the floor. Locals routinely brought chickens and other animals onto the bus with them. It was all surreal, offering glimpses of Central American life we hadn't seen even in movies.

Early in the journey, when a rattletrap bus we were riding creaked to a stop in the middle of a small town, Brett jumped down. He gathered our gear into a pile while I negotiated our fare with a man beside the driver. I

Jock Bradley

Tao is one of my closest friends even though I'm almost twice his age. When I met Tao, he was eighteen, and I was thirty-six. I didn't have the patience for an eighteen-year-old back then, but he never was eighteen, so to speak. His mother once said it right: He was born an "old soul."

didn't like the way the man was demanding more than originally agreed on, nor did I seem to be getting anywhere with my very poor Spanish.

Suddenly, I heard a *thunk*. The noise made me whip my head around a split second before the bus's motor roared into action (creating the sound I had heard), nearly throwing me off balance. The driver had shut the door and was accelerating forward with a hardened face. The filthy rear window framed Brett's mouth hanging open and his arms limp by his sides. I glanced quickly at the bus's rear door, my body stiffening. There, a bruiser of a man stood and placed his body in front of the door. I knew that back door was my best chance of escape, so I ran toward him. He smirked as he pushed down on the door handle, but I put all my strength into pulling it up, figuring whoever was stronger would win. That's when the fare-taker charged down the aisle and grabbed me from behind around the waist. As he tried to pull me backward, I muscled the

Back then, he was up and coming, starting to get name recognition. He was becoming known in the Northwest and just starting to get attention nationally. My first impression on meeting this eighteen-year-old kid was that he was going to use kayaking as a vehicle for something much more important.

handle up, grabbed the side of the open door, and pulled myself out of my tackler's grip. From there, I jumped out of the moving bus onto the road.

It might not have been good enough for an Indiana Jones scene, but it bought me my freedom. Brett and I chalked it up to another day in the life of adventuring in Central America. Of course, looking back, I'm amazed at how cavalier we were about the whole experience. But then again I may look at it the same way now.

Unfortunately, the rivers turned out to be only half as exciting as the bus rides, so we journeyed down to Honduras, kayaked there a little, carried on to the Bay Islands and Belize, and finally turned up in Guatemala again. There, we left the kayaks with a contact and spent another few months playing ordinary tourists. By then, we'd paddled somewhere between fifteen and twenty rivers. Like all kayakers visiting Third World countries, we'd learned the hard way that the difficulty in finding access points meant far more searching for rivers than actual paddling. Still, I was pretty proud of the fact that my two thousand dollars had lasted me six months. By January 1998, both Brett and I were ready to hit the road north. We bused all the way back up to California, where I said adios and joined Osho, my dad, Grandma Doreen, and others for a family reunion.

For a few months after that, I paddled in Washington while sharing a place with paddling buddies. That's when I met Jock Bradley, a professional photographer who would soon figure into my life and career in a major way. I also started hanging out with Josh Bechtel, someone I'd known since ninth grade.

Following those months in Washington, I did a semester of college in California before transferring to Ashland, Oregon. Meanwhile, I was showing my video clips of the Mexican trip wherever a gathering of paddlers seemed interested. At one get-together in California, I met Dan Gavere, a freestyle kayak racer who'd become one of the first to round up enough sponsors to make a living at paddling.

"Wow," Dan remarked after I'd shut off the video player during a paddlers' party. "I think that eighty-footer you paddled on the Rio Tomata is a world record."

"Seriously?" I asked. I'd kayaked the waterfall because it had looked challenging. I had no idea eighty feet would make it a world record. That's how out of touch I was with the paddling scene at the time. That night, I got to thinking. Could I use the footage to win sponsors and work myself into a position where I could really, truly live off kayaking? Not just marginally, like Dan, but in comfort? I loved the idea of making a living paddling, but I didn't want to end up in my mid-thirties with nothing to show for it. I couldn't live on memories alone.

When I raised this question with friends, they laughed. Never been done, they reminded me. Sport's not big enough, bro. Don't waste your time. Media don't even know who we are. Not a chance. Quit being a dreamer. Who do you think you are, anyway? With every "no," of course, I became more determined to prove them wrong.

What whitewater kayaking lacked in participants, it made up for in intrigue out there in television-land. Kayaks plunging off waterfalls made for exciting viewing. Network execs might not know a thing about our sport, but they liked the way death-defying water shots grabbed viewer attention. Here I was, studying marketing yet really wanting to paddle full-time. I became convinced I could fuse the two interests. I believed that with time and effort, I could take my sport to places it hadn't yet been. I became intent on going pro. Big-time. Well, at least big-time by my standards.

THE TAO OF MARKETING

"Celebrity sportspersons . . . have become intertwined with
the industry of extreme sports itself."

—Robert E. Rinehart,
To the Extreme: Alternative Sports, Inside and Out

was sitting in a business class. The teacher was droning on about marketing. The ugly metal desks weren't the most ergonomic in the world; they certainly weren't invented for a daydreaming athlete. A kayak seat may not be any cushier, but that's sure where I'd rather have been.

"Tao Berman," the teacher's voice cut into my thoughts. "Can you give the class examples of brands that have such major brand awareness, everyone knows them? Besides Campbell's Soup, as I was saying."

"Campbell's Soup? I've never heard of Campbell's Soup." I pretended not to hear some sniggers from the back of the room.

The instructor paused. His eyebrows arched upward. "What do you mean? Your mom never fed you Campbell's Soup when you were growing up?"

"No."

More sniggers, as disbelief in the instructor's eyes slowly turned to amused amazement. I refused to be embarrassed. I'd been in this situation so many times before. Pop culture and the Bermans never hung out together. Our family didn't have a television until I was twelve or thirteen. When I was young, our family ate food from our mountaintop garden, and my mom probably wouldn't have bought Campbell's Soup even if the firm had opened its first Eastern Washington outlet next door. Both my parents emphasized the importance of healthy eating, and I think I'm a better athlete for it.

"Well anyway," the instructor continued, grinning, "the point is, successful companies build a brand from the ground up by offering consistent satisfaction and improvement, and playing things right so that distribution and media exposure eventually elevate them to a household name."

My thoughts wandered to more important things. For months after my Central America trip, I'd showed my videos around, approaching sponsors and being approached by sponsors. I was stockpiling sponsors, dreaming of what life could be if I reached a certain threshold of sponsorship. Build a brand from the ground up, offer consistent satisfaction and improvement, and play things right so that distribution and media exposure eventually elevate you to a household name.

Lilly

Tao has always been very friendly and outgoing and able to walk up and say, "Hey, my name is Tao. What's yours?"

If I could make just eight thousand dollars a year, I thought, *I could kayak full-time.* I could do photo shoots and compete for little or no prize money as I built a brand and created awareness of it. More money would come later.

I was enjoying studying marketing at Southern Oregon University in Ashland. I was getting A's and B's for the most part, but that's not where my heart was.

If I want to make it as an athlete, I reflected, *I have one chance: when I'm young, now.* If it doesn't work out, I can always return to college.

Then came momentary doubts. Pursue paddling full-time? Everyone was telling me I couldn't make a career of it, that I was going to kill myself by trying to push the sport too far. But at that point in my life, barely nineteen, I had four sponsors: Pyranha kayaks, Werner Paddles, Stohlquist paddling tops, and Oakley sunglasses. I was making less than ten thousand dollars a year, but I had built a reputation in the Pacific Northwest as someone pushing the envelope of the sport, and I was rapidly gaining the eye of national media. (I was also fortunate in that Grandma Doreen and Grandpa Joe paid for all my schooling.)

My connection with Pyranha had come about pretty much by happenstance. Jock Bradley, a photographer and active whitewater kayaker, was paddling about one hundred fifty days a year back then, although he always described himself as a "fearful Class V boater." We'd met paddling, of course, and he briefly served as a Pyranha rep. When Britain-based Pyranha air-freighted him an Ina Zone kayak to photograph, he phoned me.

"Need a paddler to shoot on the river in a new boat," he said.

"I'm your man," I replied. It sounded like a good opportunity. After that, Jock started shooting me a lot, if not for kayak and outdoor gear companies, then for paddling shots in general. At thirty-six, he was an established photographer with a background in shooting corporate ad campaigns. He also had a passion for shooting whitewater—in both the photographic and sport senses. His paddling photos were the best I'd ever seen. He was also a really decent and fun guy I admired and enjoyed being around. So, despite the age gap between us, we quickly developed a mutually beneficial business relationship that has lasted more than a decade, with me often helping him sell photos as my own influence grew.

Early on, too, we evolved from business and paddling buddies to solid friends. One of his passions was cooking, and I was always an appreciative taster. I learned a lot from Jock, even about relationships; watching his and other friends' marriages falter contributed to my wariness of long-term commitment.

While Jock's still photos helped me grow my career early on, so did the videography talents of Eric Link, a longtime expert whitewater paddler. Like Jock, Eric met me as an eighteen-year-old, up-and-coming extreme paddler and shot me on occasion. And, like Jock, Eric soon found his shots of my river exploits expanding his own reputation and video sales. I was an "add in" on the first Twitch video, but after that, he concentrated more heavily on capturing what I was doing, which grew into five videos in the now legendary Twitch series.

By the time I'd finished my second year at Southern Oregon University, I'd progressed from four to six sponsors, and they where paying me a little more (although still not much). I achieved this by applying my marketing studies to myself—in other words, taking a business approach to my career.

I looked at myself as a product: I needed people to know who Tao Berman was. I knew that all products have a shelf life and guessed that mine might be fifteen years. I figured I'd have a growth stage (becoming recognized), a maturity phase (being established), and a decline (where things increasingly failed to go as planned, a scenario I haven't met yet). Having chosen to study marketing over two other interests—law and sales—I embraced negotiating my own contracts and doing my own promotion. It allowed me to use my mind rather than just my muscles; I'd quickly get bored as an athlete only.

Once I resolved to make whitewater kayaking my career, I studied what other people in the sport were doing right and wrong, and vowed to take what had been done well and build on it. I knew that whitewater

Eric Link

I started out by videotaping rafting trips. By the time Tao was eighteen, I'd seen some videotapes of him and knew he was a good paddler. I first met him when he phoned up and invited me to run Ernie's Canyon on the North Fork of the Snoqualmie River with him. He'd heard from his friends that I was a good paddler, and he wanted to "check out the competition." He had even more of a chip on his shoulder then than now; he's mellowed a bit.

He convinced me the canyon was at a good water level. I'd never been on it, but he said he'd run it a lot. When we got to the put-in, he got this concerned look on his face and said, "It's a little higher than I thought." We went down it anyway. The high water was making my boat do tail stands through a lot of the drops. He asked me to run some of the drops first so that I could videotape him.

My first impression of him was that he was really cocky. (He's changed a lot since.) I also concluded that he was a

kayaking was a small sport and that I'd need to do more than promote myself in the kayaking industry if I was going to make a good living kayaking.

really good boater and took things on like a tiger—he took on some big whitewater for sure.

Not long after that, I was videotaping some Dagger team members who'd come to town. A clothing company was shooting them at the same time, and they ended up liking my footage better, so they invited me to shoot them on an upcoming trip to Montana. Before they left, Tao dropped in, and I shot him on Icicle Creek and Tumwater Canyon.

As a result of the Big Timber Creek, Montana, footage I got from the Dagger guys, I put a teaser together. With that, we ended up getting sponsorship money, so I took the Dagger guys to Mexico. I returned with enough material for a video, and Tao suggested I add his Mexico footage to it. That became the first of five Twitch videos (now famous among whitewater paddlers). After that, Tao really liked what I'd done and stayed with me; I became his main videographer.

I figured if I started attracting more mainstream media coverage, then larger, out-of-industry sponsors might start taking an interest in me.

At that time, no kayakers were making good money from kayaking. Some were sponsored to the point they could enjoy kayaking as a lifestyle, but they weren't making enough to save for retirement. What they were earning was a far cry from what athletes in more popular sports such as surfing, baseball, basketball, skateboarding, and hockey were pulling down. Dan Gavere was one paddling star who came before me, and he was definitely living the life: traveling the world, shooting videos, and winning events. There were others, including Clay Wright and Eric Jackson, but Dan truly pioneered the concept of professional kayaker.

At the time, and mostly to this day, kayakers were a pretty frugal and spotlight-shunning lot. They didn't rack up much in the way of expenses; if they traveled, they lived on next to nothing. Although I was perfectly capable of doing the same, my goal was to punch past this scenario and get paid enough to kayak that I wouldn't have to take on a "real job" and restrict paddling to weekends. I also didn't want to retire from the sport in my mid-thirties, broke. I wanted to be financially set for life.

As more and more sponsors showed interest, I did all that was necessary to be a good and reliable "product," to give sponsors good value for their investment. That's all any professional athletes are, whether they like to admit it or not: products.

Because I was a pioneer among paddlers in this regard, detractors were quick to call me a "sellout" and "egotist." As a marketing student, I could shrug off these words. I knew there was a fine line between promoting oneself and being perceived as self-centered, and, predictably, there existed a number of paddlers not ready or willing to have their sport "discovered." Especially if the newfound attention seemed overly focused on one paddler-come-lately in only one facet of the sport. Whitewater, after

Having some fun at a Red Bull sales meeting in Hawaii. I'm the one lying on the ground.

all, embraces everything from slalom and freestyle competition to commercial rafting, none of which are on most media's radar. If the inroads I was making to the press had potential upside for these other aspects of the sport, I could understand why no one was eager to thank me for it. There were times I probably attracted 70 to 80 percent of the sport's mainstream media coverage. It's lonely at the forefront and, as I was soon to learn, even lonelier at the top. But it was a small price to pay for being able to do something I loved so much.

Athletes in less-popular sports dare not dream of turning their hobby into a career. And athletes in more-popular sports can afford to leave the promotion to an agent and concentrate on their performances, thereby escaping criticism for self-promotion. But I knew where my sport stood and what I had to do. I had to serve as my own public-relations consultant and follow a tried-and-true formula: build brand recognition of my name and feats, keep myself available to media to keep my sponsors happy, and turn in consistently newsworthy results.

I was lucky in that the media were kind of intrigued by an eighteen-year-old kid pitching stories by himself. I could be a little crass and unrefined; they expected that of a young athlete doing first descents and his own marketing. Some of my early mistakes may not have hurt me as much as they would now. But looking back on some of my interviews, I'm pretty embarrassed by just how cocky I was.

All this was (and is) in the name of kayaking for a living, the not-so-secret dream of most hard-core young paddlers—including (if not especially) many of my detractors.

However, I've also had kind and unexpected support from people I hardly know. Back in 1997, around the time Jock was starting to shoot me, I was kayaking in Washington with a Pyranha-sponsored paddler. After watching me run rapids he was portaging, he returned to the eastern United States and told a U.S. Pyranha exec, "Hey, there's this kid out West who's just nuts. It won't be long before you see him everywhere."

Clearly, this paddler didn't feel threatened by me. Back then, I was busy doing first descents in the Cascades with my friends, seeking out the most difficult water we could run. We led a pretty sheltered life; we paid no attention to what kayakers were doing around the world. But when the Pyranha paddler started talking me up on the other side of the country, I started getting calls from companies that wanted me to paddle their boats. My world was opening up.

As a former marketing student, I take a different approach than many paddlers. I try to look at matters from the sponsors' perspective— try to put myself in their shoes. Truth be told, they couldn't care less what I want; they just want to sell product. I figure if I can outline how their giving me something will help them sell it, then I optimize my chances of getting on board. It sounds so simple, but so many would-be-sponsored athletes look first at what they want.

I also see a lot of athletes going for whatever company pays them the most. Or they spend one year with one sponsor and the next with another. That's not seeing the big picture. Once you've developed and built a relationship, there's more to be gained by both athlete and sponsor if it lasts. Both fans and sponsors are less likely to see you as a sellout.

By my second year in Ashland, I was so busy with my paddling career that I had to make a decision: did I want to continue college and finish my marketing degree or go with the success already pouring in? I ended up quitting school because I wanted to do one thing at 100 percent rather than divide my energies. I knew that I had only one life and that while I could always return to school, I'd never be able to return to my physical prime and this high level of interest from potential sponsors. I didn't want to look back and wonder what I'd have made out of my kayaking career if only I hadn't stayed the academic course. I had to seize the moment and explore what I could do.

Looking back, I have no regrets. I had six or seven sponsors at the time, which I consider a full roster. That meant I had enough companies supplying me gear, money, and travel expenses that I was in a position to paddle full-time. I also didn't have to keep looking for more sponsors. Acquire too many, and you can't serve any of them properly. (Not to mention you can't fit all their stickers on your boat.) In fact, with few exceptions, I've stayed with that early list for nearly a decade. I don't believe in dropping or acquiring sponsors on whim. I'm big on loyalty, and as I said, I believe that long-term relationships offer the best benefit to everyone all around.

Driving the rock crawler at a Red Bull party near Las Vegas

Today, I earn around two hundred fifty thousand dollars in a good year. This doesn't count the gear and other benefits, such as Subaru cars, KTM motorcycles, and so on. My current list of sponsors is as follows: Red Bull energy drink, Timberland outdoor gear, Mion shoes, Dagger kayaks, Voz Sports helmets, Stohlquist paddling gear, and AT Paddles.

I've been with Red Bull since 1999, when my career was just getting going. They encouraged an acquaintance of mine to have me contact them. Unlike other firms, Red Bull sponsors only one or two top people in any sport, and those sports range from Formula 1 auto racing to street luge. Red Bull has several hundred athletes worldwide and generally tries to find an athlete early in his career, then stick with him for the duration. That makes Red Bull and me a great fit. Red Bull is one of the best sponsors an athlete can hope to have. The company allows me to go out and do what I do best, without micromanaging me or my schedule. I have good relationships with a lot of people at Red Bull and hope to be a Red Bull athlete for the rest of my career. Even if one of their competitors offered me 50 percent more, I doubt I'd switch.

Because of confidentiality clauses, I can't reveal exactly how much each sponsor pays me or what it requires in return. But I'll explain roughly how it works. Usually, a sponsor will supply gear and a salary, and in return I use its products and place its logos on my kayak or apparel. Sometimes, a sponsor will ask me to make an appearance somewhere or carry only its logo on my boat. One might ask me, for instance, to hold up my water bottle with its logo on it for everyone to see when I stand on a podium. Or it will ask me to wear its logo-decked hat. Some sponsors spell those requirements out in such detail that reading the contract can make an athlete's head spin.

Just imagine the seconds immediately following a race win, when spectators, reporters, and others are coming up to you. You arrive at the podium only to realize that your cap is askew and your water bottle's back in your boat. It's hard to keep it all straight. On the other hand, if I'm stepping up to the podium or giving a television interview, I want to give back to my sponsors. I want to have the bottle in hand and cap on straight.

In general, I look for sponsors who trust me to do the best I can and know that my track record for "giving back" is solid; they don't push nitpicky clauses at me and don't demand so many trips to their headquarters that I can hardly find time to paddle. I also look for companies full of people easy to work with. I like sponsors who give me whatever product I need and don't ask for media incentives. When you agree to work with media incentives, you have to track every article recently published on you and debate with the sponsor such petty details as the size of the logo and why it didn't make it into a recently published photo. I don't have time for that.

One sponsor I'm no longer with because of such issues is Teva. Teva did a lot for my career, but it tried to control my schedule to such a degree that it seemed too much like work and wasn't fun anymore. Once, Teva executives demanded that I fly to California for a sales meeting even though I had another commitment. The meeting was at a swank resort in Santa Monica, and that's where all the sales staff were staying. But at the end of the meeting, the team manager drove ten of us lowly kayakers out of the resort to a crappy hotel.

"Shows how cheap they always are with their athletes," I remember thinking as the van lurched toward the hotel. "They think we'll take this because we don't know any better." For me, that was the last straw. I decided I'd rather have no shoe sponsor than stay with Teva. The

Jamie Simon, Red Bull marketing

He's definitely worth every penny. He's very much of a self-marketing machine, constantly accommodating and willing to work with media, well branded. Tao gets a lot of exposure; he's constantly in magazines and newspapers. He's also a huge impact on the local market in Hood River [Oregon], where he lives. He's a real trendsetter in the world of pro kayaking. He does really well at the business side as well as performance side. Accountability is his best asset. He's great about providing monthly updates that keep track of his performance. It would be great if other athletes sent results to their sponsors. That's something we really appreciate from Tao. When he gets exposure, he makes sure he gets a copy of it to us so we don't have to track it down. On a scale of one to ten, he is a nine.

company had been making unreasonable demands for a while, and I chose not to renew my contract.

On the other hand, one of the biggest negotiating mistakes I made involved Teva. Early on, while negotiating my own contract with the company for shoes, I asked about getting stock options. I figured it was a win–win proposition; I'd try harder to promote the brand if my incentive was tied to stock. The response was to offer me less money and more stock options, which didn't sit well with me at the time, so I went with relatively few stock options and more money up-front. I wasn't thinking of the big picture. When the stock went up several hundred percent shortly thereafter, I realized that my shortsighted decision had just cost me a couple hundred

Christian Knight

A few years ago, I'd just published a guidebook. It was very small, and the publisher had printed it on cheap paper. So I was kind of insecure about the book-signing event. I'm not used to people coming to see me. The bookstore did a lousy job of marketing it. I mean, this was a small town where I'd been a reporter, and it was Octoberfest. They'd given me this little table and no display. After two or three hours, I hadn't managed to sell a single book. Then Tao stopped by to see me and said, "This sucks." He convinced me to move the table outside and challenged me to a contest over which of us could sell more books. Then he started photographing me and drawing people's attention to us. I felt on the spot and awkward about the whole thing, but we sold almost fifteen books, mostly because of him. It was cool of him to do that. He takes this obsessive interest in his friends. The event went from being a lame time to being a great memory. Afterwards, we went out and got drunk at Octoberfest.

thousand dollars. Even though the stock options I had did well, I realized I'd made a mistake—or, more accurately, learned a valuable lesson.

Regularly, I go on the Web and check out my sponsors' lines of products. I almost never go shopping for clothes; I just order whatever looks cool from these online pages. If it turns out to be uncomfortable, I won't wear it. I'll ask for something else, and I'll give the people at the company my feedback, which they appreciate for product development. Sometimes, a company doesn't innovate at a rate I like or my tastes change. Werner still makes a great paddle, and I like some of the people who work there, but at one point, I felt it had stopped being progressive. I was more impressed with what AT Paddles was doing. Werner is one of the few early sponsors I changed.

Another was Kavu. At first, I loved wearing Kavu clothing, but then my sense of style changed, and even though I had no clothing-company replacement in mind, I chose not to renew my contract. I'm at a point where I can do that. I really enjoy my career, and I like my sponsors' products. If it stops being fun for me or I don't like something I'm promoting, then I figure it's time to change.

One sponsor I canceled but sometimes wish I hadn't is Pyranha Kayaks. I always felt their boats were great, but the company is based in England, and my relationship at the time was with the U.S. importer. When the importer went out of business, the U.K. office didn't call me right away to assure me that the athlete program would continue to run as it had. I felt the company would have done that if it were serious about the program; I felt unsure about my future there. So I cut ties when, in fact, the company has continued to thrive and produce quality boats. Maybe I should have been more patient and seen how things played out. But I can't complain, because I'm really happy with the kayaks that my current boat sponsor makes.

Sometimes I'm flown to meetings to advise company designers on how to make a better paddle, paddling jacket, boat, or whatever. This applies to almost all my sponsoring companies. Their goal is to be progressive and stay ahead of their competitors, and their athletes' feedback helps them accomplish this. I'm glad to be part of that process because it gives me better products to use. But I'm a bit more comfortable on rivers than in boardrooms.

Once, while I was at a Dagger team dinner with thirty people, I started rocking back in my chair as the conversation turned to upcoming marketing strategies. Imagine my embarrassment when the chair tipped too far. There I was on the floor of a private room in a restaurant, company executives all around laughing till the table shook. Oh, well; I guess I'll always be more of a restless athlete than a desk jockey.

In general, a sponsor that asks me to place a two-inch sticker on my boat will pay me less than a sponsor that asks for an eight-inch sticker. Some will ask me to make appearances; others make no demands beyond the stickers.

I don't chase the highest number of dollars. I look for companies whose products I like and I feel good about promoting. This isn't merely a matter of feeling good. For me, the right product can maximize my safety, while the wrong product can contribute to injury or death. I also don't want more than seven or so major sponsors; I don't want my kayak looking like something from the NASCAR circuit. Even now, I have an arrangement with Stohlquist not to place its logo on my boat; instead, it's just on my paddle top. Beyond my seven major sponsors, I have some minor ones not so directly related to my kayaking career. For instance, Subaru supplies me with a car and KTM with a motorcycle. TaylorMade recently gave me a two-thousand-five-hundred-dollar set of golf clubs, and Giant gave me a four-thousand-dollar mountain bike. They figure their products will show up in features about me, and they're right. When I'm doing cross-training, the media like to shoot me on my mountain bike, road bike, or motorcycles.

Of course, I can't have two sponsors that compete with one another. Because Red Bull is known for its energy drinks, I can never be

Lilly

I admire his ability to go after what he wants. That's very rare. He has the ability to think, "I'm going to go get that, and it doesn't matter what I have to do to attain it."

Once when he was around twelve years old, he wanted a Nintendo, so he went and sat in front of Safeway with all his used toys, determined to sell them to whoever walked in that door. And he did it. He sold all his toys and made enough money to buy that Nintendo. He could talk you into whatever he wanted to. He was a great salesman from the youngest age. That's just his personality.

sponsored by Go Fast or another energy-drink company. Once, I turned down a Land Rover because I already had a Subaru. But there are definitely perks to being an established athlete!

When a sponsor supplies me with a travel budget, I use it to travel to a videotaping. Naturally, the more I appear in magazines, in newspapers, online, or on television, the happier sponsors are. But given kayaking's low profile overall, it's not hard to find myself bumping up against the ceiling called "overexposure." I realize, though, that every sponsored athlete would like to have the problem of hitting the saturation point. Once, *Paddler* magazine ran the tongue-in-cheek line, "This is a Tao and E. J.–free issue." (E. J. is a high-profile freestyle kayaker.) What could I do but chuckle?

Kayaking is not yet a mature industry. If surfer Kelly Slater does something interesting, a ton of magazines fall over themselves to write about it. That's way less true for whitewater kayakers, although if someone writes something about me on a paddling forum, it certainly inspires lots of responses.

When I was in my teens, it was common to run across people who didn't know what a kayak was. I haven't had that response in years. In fact, in some ways, the sport has more appeal to mainstream viewers than to participants themselves. When NBC's *Dateline* did a feature on me, the announcers referred to the arresting shots of the difficult whitewater as "eye candy." Anyone can appreciate watching a colorful kayak plunge over a beautiful but terrifying-looking waterfall. Any kid can relate to the element of danger and fear of the unknown. Extreme kayaking has sex appeal; it's fun to watch.

BUSINESS AND MISCHIEF

"Pushing, striving and stretching are essential components of being successful in the business world or being a success in life."

—Dan Jelinski, business consultant, speaker, and author of *Be the Leader They Love!*

Cameras, film, action: It never ceases to amaze me how many people and hours it takes to capture just minutes of viewable action.

Once, I was being shot for a Teva print ad campaign. Teva execs wanted a nighttime head shot of me looking intense and focused. They flew something like twenty-five people to Arizona and waited for nightfall. Several people were in charge of keeping a fire stoked behind me. Another person's job was to splash water on my face. There was a photographer, caterers, art directors, ad-agency representatives, and assistants upon assistants to all of the above.

Another time, I was involved in doing an ad campaign for an energy bar. They flew me to California for a shot of what I see when I look over my shoulder at the river. Not a shot of me or my face, note, but of what I see when I look around. They hired a stunt double for me. He sat in the kayak with his head turned just so and his hands on the paddle. Someone was in charge of holding the stern of his kayak against the bank as the photographer leaned in over his shoulder to determine the best angle. I hung out at the food-service wagon, watching in semi-disbelief.

"Tao! We're ready for you," the photographer eventually shouted. Into the kayak I went, and the photographer shot over my shoulder for thirty seconds. Out of the kayak I came, ready to accommodate the person assigned to drive me back to the airport.

I couldn't help thinking that Jock and I could have done all this in less than thirty seconds, with one assistant if we'd really wanted to splurge!

The people involved in such shoots typically know little or nothing about whitewater paddling. Plus, they're often highly unionized—resulting in an army to do a soldier's work, in my opinion—and they tend to walk around as if insurance companies are watching over their shoulder. I've done this for long enough that I understand and cooperate, but can anyone blame me for retaining a sense of humor about it? In fact, my fellow paddlers and I have developed a reputation for pulling practical jokes on set.

Once, I was doing an interview for a morning show, and the producers decided they wanted the host—a young, fun-loving, but urban guy—to be shot sitting in a kayak next to my kayak in the water. I suggested that he demonstrate a roll.

"Think I could?" he asked, clearly tempted.

I knew he didn't have a prayer—a person needs lots of instruction and practice to pull off a roll—but I figured I'd have some fun with his naïveté. "Sure," I encouraged him. "I'll show you how before we go live."

"All right!" he agreed, being a good sport.

"You hold your paddle like this, lean until you go over, then flip your hips like so. Voila, you're up."

"Got it!" he said, still sitting upright, his dry hair perfectly coiffed.

The cameras rolled, we went live, and we chatted for the viewers before I challenged him to go for it. Over he went, and then . . . nothing. He came out of his kayak and surfaced wet, cold, and choking on water, but grinning. The production crew was laughing heartily.

Another time, prior to meeting for a shoot in Chile, an art director phoned me numerous times to discuss my wardrobe. He felt it was important for me to bring what was required, as it would be a real problem getting different clothes in Chile. When I actually walked onto the set, I was purposely wearing an entirely mismatched outfit in all the colors he hadn't approved. The photographer, who had dealt with me enough to know I was a prankster, moved away to hold his sides. The art director freaked out until he caught his staff snickering. It was beautiful.

That evening, we all went to a restaurant for dinner. As one waiter delivered a plate of cheese cubes, each with its own toothpick, another waiter placed a plate of butter squares near me. When the art director wasn't looking, I quickly plucked the toothpicks from the cheese cubes and shoved them into the butter squares, then passed him the butter plate.

A strange look appeared on his face as he popped the first butter pat into his mouth. The rest of the dinner guests roared. As payback, I got a wake-up call from the hotel at four o'clock the next morning. When no one would fess up as to who'd done it, I delivered 4 a.m. wake-up calls to everyone the morning after that.

I guess I'm a bad influence on the paddlers who accompany me on trips, because sometimes they're the instigators of practical jokes. Once, a bunch of us, including my buddy Josh, were in Argentina videotaping the run of a hundred-foot sliding waterfall that spilled into a lake. One of the paddlers, named Devon, was someone I quickly sized up as lacking

Osho

Whether it's kayaking, working your way up the corporate ladder, or starting your own business, at the end of the day Tao has the necessary qualities for success. He's persistent, he plans, he really thinks things through. He's pragmatic; he doesn't get too lost in numbers.

the required skills. He wouldn't take my suggestion that he not do the falls, so I waited at the bottom, truly concerned he was going to crash big. On shore, more safety guys waited, one of them Devon's friend Ben.

Devon climbed into his kayak, and I watched him slide over the first ten feet of the falls. Then his kayak flipped upside down, and he did the last ninety feet on his head and side. As he splashed into the lake, we all assumed he was hurt. The only question in my mind was how badly.

Josh and I were the first to reach him. When we determined that, miraculously, he was unhurt, Josh said, "Hey, how about you pretend to be hurt? If anyone asks you a question, answer, 'Mom, is that you?'"

Devon chuckled and did a thumbs-up. Josh grinned at me, knowing I wasn't about to object. The second we dragged him up onto shore, Devon started rolling around on the ground and moaning. Ben rushed to his side and said, "Devon, Devon. How many fingers am I holding up?"

Devon squinted at his friend's upheld hand and said, "Mom, is that you?"

Ben leapt up and sprinted for the first-aid kit in the motorboat. He slowed only when he realized that Josh and I had fallen to the ground laughing. It was mean, yes, but, again, it sure was funny. In my line of work, there are so many close calls and near disasters that we don't take them too seriously.

Josh the practical joker once played one on me. Driving a logging road in Canada, he braked when a black bear lumbered across in front of us. I hopped out to walk to the road's edge where I'd last seen it. Josh picked up a big rock and tossed it into the bushes beside me. I whirled around with my fists up, ready to fight that bear, only to see Josh and my friends hooting with laughter. I felt like such an idiot.

While I've developed a modest fan base in North America, never have I met fans like I have in Japan. At races they throng me like I'm a movie star and sometimes even ask me to sign their cars. Having noticed how they watch my every move and try to mimic me, I couldn't resist playing a practical joke the day after I'd won the Japanese Open for freestyle in 2000. I was holding a clinic, during which I was in charge of taking ten Japanese paddlers down a river and teaching them paddling technique en route. The night before the clinic, I bought a package of Oreo cookies and a container of wasabi, a fiery-hot Japanese condiment. I opened each cookie and replaced the white circle of frosting with a heaping pile of wasabi. During the next day's luncheon stop, as the caterers passed out food to everyone, I produced my "gift." The paddlers studied how I popped an Oreo into my mouth whole (mine was one I hadn't messed with) and did the same. I watched their eyes grow large and their heads jerk around to take in one another's reactions. When they saw me laughing, they joined in, aware I'd played a joke on them.

Outside my own little circle of friends, I'm often perceived as being serious, but clearly, I'm a big prankster. When a friend who'd never been out of the United States joined me for a shoot in the Philippines, I couldn't resist targeting him. I told him there was a condition in those parts called "crotch rot," a painful rash that takes over your private parts and can be prevented only by applying an ointment every day. Every night after that, my fellow paddlers and I pretended to put on this ointment, influencing our more gullible friend to do so too.

"Remember," I reminded him, "if it burns when you put it on, you've caught crotch rot."

The fifth day of this routine, we switched our friend's ointment bottle for one containing Bengay. We heard his screams from the bathroom even before he came running out, holding his hands over his genitals. He was running in circles around the courtyard of our quarters, shouting, "I've got crotch rot! It's burning!"

We were hiding and trying to silence our laughter. When he finally calmed down and came inside, he begged us to tell him how to rid himself of the condition. We solemnly advised him that the only way to get rid of it was to continue to apply the ointment twice daily.

Dad

Tao's biggest accomplishment is the way he has created a lifestyle for himself, building on his sports accomplishments and business skills. His character is the glue that holds the package together. He has always been pretty damn cocky from as far back as I remember. That has always been a trait of his, and it doesn't seem to have abated any. From a very early age—four or five—he demonstrated enough business savvy that I always knew he was going to go into some form of business.

Two times each day after that, we heard the poor fellow yelping with pain. The joke ended when the bottle of Bengay broke and we owned up. Our friend heaved a big sigh and said, "Would've been a lot funnier if you'd done it to someone else."

One of my favorite practical jokes of all time was played the winter of 2007 in Chile when we where photographing a print ad campaign. About thirty people were there to shoot me kayaking some extreme whitewater. One staffer was a New Yorker named Nadina who knew nothing about whitewater but had been assigned to do "risk assessment." That meant she followed me like a shadow, trying to stop me from doing anything too risky.

Christian Knight

Tao's incredible talent beyond kayaking is that he is one of the few people of this world who can see himself as a product—a very, very good product everyone will want to have.

When Jock Bradley and I spied a tree limb hanging well out from the top of a forty-foot waterfall I was thinking about paddling for the shoot, we decided it was the perfect scouting place.

"You're not climbing that without ropes and harnesses," Nadina warned.

I smiled at her and scrambled right out onto the limb. I looked down to the still pool at the bottom of the waterfall, which I'd already determined was deep and clear of rocks, and I asked Jock, "Do you think if I jump from here, that would freak out Nadina?"

"Oh yeah," he said with a conspiratorial grin.

I handed him my wallet, cell phone, and watch, and climbed a little farther out on the branch, ignoring Nadina's entreaties. It was fifty feet from there to the water. With no warning, I hurled myself out of the tree. The scream she emitted as I free-fell was music to my ears. She totally freaked out. It was even more satisfying than the clean, cool landing below.

The next day, Nadina was pacing up and down the shore, twisting her hands as she peered at the Class III rapid I was about to paddle. The art director, Jock, and Jock's assistant were giving me a final briefing when Jock's assistant suggested that I capsize in the rapid and pretend I couldn't roll up, to scare Nadina again.

I paddled down the first portion of the rapid, then flipped over in a benign piece of the turbulence—benign-looking if you knew anything about whitewater, nasty-looking if you didn't. Instead of doing a quick roll, I stayed upside down for about thirty seconds, my hands pounding on the bottom of my boat. Jock yelled at the safety crew to throw me a rescue line. About the time it landed near my boat, I rolled up, grinning from ear to ear, and blew Nadina a big kiss.

She was livid. She was beet-red. It wasn't funny to her then, and it wasn't funny to her hours later. But the whole production crew thought it was hilarious. She stopped speaking to Jock's assistant for twenty-four hours. She wasn't able to stop speaking to Jock or me, since we were the stars, so she leveled her revenge on Jock's assistant. I'll always remember Nadina.

The market machinery of shoots can generate its own kind of pressure, too. The television show *Stunt Junkies* on Discovery Channel once flew a producer and me to Superior Falls in Michigan just to get a visual for a potential shoot. Once I'd said yes, that I wanted to kayak it, that put the big ball into motion. By the time a huge crew accompanied us to the site, here's what I had hanging over me: a contract that said if I backed out for anything less than certainty that I would get hurt, it would cost me $50,000. As it turned out, the water had dropped, and we needed to reevaluate whether it was safe. But I made the objective decision that it was still good to go, and the crew ended up getting the shot everybody wanted.

Would I let that kind of pressure sway a decision if I didn't deem something safe? No way. There is a very small line between a perfect route and a disaster. If I don't think I can pull it off, I will not get into my boat. I'm a paddler first and video star second. I knew how to call things on a river long before cameras became part of my life, and I'll know how to call them long after networks disappear from my life.

People who don't know me assume otherwise. They figure now that I've paddled a 98.4-foot drop, I'll feel I "have to" paddle a 100-foot drop to keep my reputation, my sponsors, and my media buzz. Hey, if I find a navigable 100-foot drop, I'll paddle it because it's there and I can't resist challenges, not because anyone's breathing down my neck. Remember, I was doing this long before I invited the media along for the ride, and I invited the media only so I could continue doing it full-time. I love pushing myself, but I have no interest in killing myself. Every risk I take is a calculated risk. Either I calculate that I can do it, or I turn my back and walk away. How else would I have gotten to where I am? I've been doing this for fifteen years with virtually no injury. End of discussion (until the next chapter, The Tao of Risk).

I turn down marketing and media opportunities, for sure. I declined to appear on the *Weakest Link* celebrity show because it requires a knack for trivia, and given the lack of television in my upbringing, I'd have ended up looking like a dumb-ass.

When asked to do a cigarette commercial, I didn't hesitate to say no. Cigarettes are terrible for people! Why would I want to promote them?

These days, I don't need to do as much self-promotion. The promotion machine has built up its own momentum. Besides, I now have an agent, and many of my sponsors have publicists working on my behalf. But I do a lot more in life than just paddle. I'm running a business: me. It's ironic, really, that I chose to paddle so I wouldn't have to do a nine-to-five job. Well, I'm paddling as often as a body can paddle, but I'm also in business, and I've had to learn business skills to keep myself paddling. But I love it, because business interests me a lot.

One person I really admire is Warren Buffett, the investor and business success guru. I've read several books by and about him. As simple as some of his advice is, it's so seldom applied. For instance, he says to find people who are good at what they do, and let them do it. That's what I've done with Jock Bradley and Eric Link. They're good at photography, and much of what I've done in my kayak has benefited them, while much of what they've done with their cameras has benefited me. I've always tried to surround myself with people I need who are better than I am at what they're doing. I owe so much to Jock and Eric, as both business associates and friends.

It was Jock who found us Lacy Falls in Canada, which turned into the NBC and *Sports Illustrated* feature. To date, I've done more than fifty first-descents around the world. There are hundreds more yet to be done, but they're getting more and more difficult to find and access. Either they're in war-torn or dangerous areas (Afghanistan, parts of Africa, and jungle regions of Colombia and the Philippines) or they're far from roads

Osho

What I admire about Tao is his discipline. He's extremely focused and disciplined and persistent. If he wants to do something, he makes it happen. He makes himself good at it if he's not good at it. He used to have a bad memory. Then he started working on it, testing himself and conditioning himself to improve in that area. He does that with a lot of things, developing and becoming noticeably better.

or trails. Tackling the latter requires lifting everything in by helicopter (expensive even for major American television networks) or embarking on a logistically nightmarish hike in. In such places, half the danger is getting to the river without getting kidnapped.

In order to run a river in the Philippines a few years ago, my group went through several layers of contacts to ensure we had the permission and protection of a particular tribe. Where we were headed, even government troops fear to tread. In fact, months before we arrived, the jeep of a government minister had accidentally struck and killed a child who'd run out into the road. When the minister refused to pay the money that the family of the child demanded, the family hacked him to pieces with a machete. In a separate incident, locals chopped off the hands of a driver who ran into a kid.

As we bumped along that same road, our driver was petrified of hitting one of the many children who ran along beside us, curious. It's likely the children had never seen kayaks before. When we finally reached the river, I enjoyed the run so much that I got ahead of some of my paddling companions. That's when I saw a group of locals gazing at me coldly from shore. There's no doubt in my mind that their stares communicated a desire to hurt me badly. The only thing stopping them was the knowledge that we had the protection of the dominant family, which would have retaliated.

As difficult as it may be to find new first descents, people such as Eric, Jock, and I find them. It's our business and our thrill.

Nowadays, Eric has his hands in many businesses, from producing sheep cheese to renting out audiovisual equipment in Wenatchee, Washington, filming weddings and Old Town Canoe DVDs, and writing songs for his band. But through all that, he still finds himself licensing ten-year-old whitewater footage to clients such as *World's Most Amazing Videos*. Or as he says, "I love it when Hollywood calls."

Teamwork is another key success factor in both business and paddling. You have to overcome obstacles, evaluate risk, trust your instincts, train your instincts, learn from your mistakes. You have to learn group dynamics, look after your support crew, and reciprocate whenever possible to those who've helped along the way. Above all, to my mind, is loyalty. Creating long-term relationships has benefited me throughout my career. I do everything I can to avoid burning a bridge.

Another lesson I've learned is how to deal with criticism. I'm in the public eye, and I see a lot of what is said about me in print. You can't please everyone, and you'll always have critics, so it's important to do what you feel is right and stick with that. I wouldn't have gotten very far if I'd made decisions based on trying to appease critics.

Perhaps last but not least is leadership. I need to know the strengths and weaknesses of each of my team members and ask of them only what plays to their strengths. I need to project confidence, because people looking up to me need to see confidence in my decisions. Leadership also means being liberal with compliments. I try my best to acknowledge and recognize people who help me. A compliment takes so little effort, yet goes so far in generating goodwill and maintaining motivation.

THE TAO OF RISK

"Risk makes our society healthier and more vibrant."

—Ron Watters,
physical-education professor and author

From tall and ribbonlike to squat and violent, waterfalls command people's attention merely for spilling water with a mesmerizing continuity. People veer off highways and clamber to viewpoints just to stare.

The day I ambled up to the lip of ninety-eight-foot Upper Johnston Canyon Falls in Banff National Park, Canada, I heard a lady on the viewing deck one hundred fifty feet away start crying. I glanced over, bemused. She seemed convinced I was about to commit suicide. The men on the deck were jostling for the best view of me. And I wasn't even in my boat yet.

I tuned out the tourists and turned my attention to a log sitting on the riverbank. Time for the videographers, photographers, and safety crew to start getting ready. Our first task was pushing logs off the falls to observe what happened to them. It may sound primitive, but it's actually the best way I've found to determine the depth of a pool at the base of a falls.

No one had ever run a ninety-eight-foot waterfall before that day: August 23, 1999. The eighty-footer I'd paddled in Mexico still stood as an unofficial world record. So no one knew how paddling off Johnston Falls might impact my body. I knew there was an outside chance it could shatter my spine even if I managed to slice cleanly and well angled into deep water at the falls' base. But before I'd even consider running this tall, thin giant, I needed to know whether the pool was deep enough and rock-free. If none of the logs we pushed over the falls shattered on impact, and if I liked when and where the logs resurfaced, I'd be closer to saying yes. Having sustained no injuries during the five years I'd been using this method of observation, I had come to trust it.

Our neoprene boots squelched on the rock as Christian and I carried small logs to the lip of the falls. As the first one took a kamikaze dive toward the eight-foot-wide lip, we scrambled to where we could train our eyes on its torpedo-like plunge into the thundering, mist-enshrouded cauldron ten stories below.

The pool swallowed it whole.

"One thousand, two thousand, three thousand, . . . " I counted under my breath as I swept my eyes from the log's entry point to well downstream of the turbulent water and back again.

"There it is!" Christian shouted.

I leapt up. "It surfaced about twenty feet downstream," I calculated enthusiastically, "meaning the pool is probably deep at the base of the falls." If a log reappears well downstream from a falls, it means it plunged deeply and traveled along the bottom of the river before resurfacing. If it pops up right away, that indicates the pool is probably shallow. Had it resurfaced quickly but in pieces, on the other hand, that would have alerted us to rocks just under the surface. Shattered logs and logs that get tumbled under water for ominous amounts of time worry kayakers.

"All in one piece," I said. "Let's do another!" Soon my helpers—all prepared to morph into film and safety crew members if I decided to run the falls—were carrying more logs to the launch spot. We were quite the spectacle for the swelling observation-deck crowd, but anyone who lingered long enough ended up getting more of an eyeful.

Like a disorderly family of lemmings, the logs we pushed into the current floated leisurely toward the lip and disappeared, one by one, as we sprinted back and forth with growing excitement.

You can't really scout a waterfall from its lower end, especially not one this height. Even where there's lower access, thick mist and roiling

water currents guard the bottom pool's secrets. Water falling that far even whips up its own wicked wind gusts. Nor can you send scuba divers into water that turbulent; they'd see nothing even if they were willing to risk their lives. The log method, to my mind, is as scientific as you can get. Not only were we assessing whether the pool was deep, obstacle-free, and without whirlpool-like recycling currents, but we also needed to ensure that the water-carved cave beside the falls' bottom wasn't sucking floating objects into it. Peering at that undercut, I had a strong hunch that the cave, not the waterfall itself, was what had claimed the lives of four of the five people who'd washed over Johnston Falls in recent history. None, as far as I knew, had gone over it on purpose.

I'm setting the world waterfall-descent record at 98.4 feet in Alberta, Canada. At the time it was about 20 feet higher than any waterfall that had been run.

photo courtesy of Tao Berman collection

In central Mexico filming a TV show for the Discovery Channel show *Stunt Junkies*. I did a first descent of this waterfall about eight years earlier and almost crashed big.

photo courtesy of Jock Bradle

Kayaking a waterfall in Chiapas, Mexico. I threw my paddle because I was landing in green water and I was concerned that the impact might break my paddle or smash me in the face with it.

photo courtesy of Jock Bradley

Training on a river near my home for my upcoming racing season. There is a direct correlation between how hard you train and how often you win, so I take my training seriously.

photo courtesy of Jock Bradle

Here I'm being filmed in Chile for a TV show on the National Geographic Adventure channel.

Being filmed for a feature that *Dateline NBC* was doing

Kayaking for a photo shoot.

photo courtesy of Jock Bradley

In Michigan filming for a show on Discovery Channel. This may not look too hard, but I'm landing in water that is only about 1.5 feet deep. And just around the corner is a 60-plus-foot waterfall.

photo courtesy of Tao Berman collectio

I looked up and down the full length of the water curtain, a sparkling ribbon against rugged, stratified, gray granite. It was a pretty waterfall if you were a tourist. But pretty is not how I think of a 150-cubic-feet-per-second flow I'm about to kayak down. I'd already calculated it'd be less than a three-second flight. And I knew that amid the faucet-like spill, I'd look as insignificant as a watermelon seed being spit to the ground. Ninety-eight-foot falls—even those barely a kayak-length wide—can make a kayaker look pretty insignificant.

By now, the observation-deck crowd had hit about a hundred milling people. Word was probably circulating that I was going to kayak it.

For a year, I'd been searching for a falls close to a hundred feet high. Then, just the day before, while filming other whitewater in Alberta, I'd gotten invited to a party where I'd overheard some ice climbers discuss their climb of this falls months earlier, in winter. When I'd asked them about the possibility of kayaking over it, they'd just looked at me as if I were out of my mind.

The very next morning, Eric visited the appropriate authorities to secure permission for paddling the creek beneath the falls. He "forgot" to mention I might do the falls, too, and the authorities didn't ask. Canada is great that way. In Canada, you can't sue anyone for being an idiot. Now, after examining the falls from every angle, I'd narrowed my list of concerns to just two.

First, the water was falling as neatly as a bridal veil except for one snag eighty-five feet down. That's where spray shot out the middle, indicating that a rock flake stuck out in the center of the flow. Hit a rock flake like that at close to fifty-five miles an hour, and there's no telling how far it'll launch you off course. I knew that if I ran the falls, I needed to avoid touching that flake at all costs. But to avoid that snag, I'd have to run the waterfall to the flake's left. And if I got too far left, a rocky shoulder that started one-third of the way down would nudge me with all the gentleness of a thousand-pound gorilla.

As for threading the slot between the gorilla's shoulder and the flake, well, did I mention that the lip over which I had to shoot was a stingy eight feet wide? My success hinged on sliding over a very precise slot of that lip and drifting not a hair left or right during my wild ride down. There was absolutely no margin for error. I had to line up my kayak so that I would fall the first eighty feet into a spot no more than three feet across.

Further, I absolutely had to hit the pool totally perpendicular, not at an angle as on Lacy. Lacy is a slide; Johnston is fully vertical, and by the time I hit Johnston's pool, I'd be going around fifty-five miles per hour. Vertical was the only way to minimize the shattering impact. If I landed in any position less than vertical, I might live, but I'd surely shatter my back.

Many kayakers have run thirty-three-foot Spirit Falls in Washington near the Oregon border. Seven have broken their backs doing so. Johnston is three times as high. I had a creative idea for maximizing my chances of staying bulletlike vertical: I planned to half-fill a milk jug with water and shove it (partially crushed for extra shock absorption) in front of my feet in the kayak. Ballast, pure and simple. A weight where I needed it in my eight-foot-one-inch-long, forty-pound plastic boat.

The kayak I chose was designed to resurface quickly, but in this instance, I actually worried it might resurface so quickly that I'd suffer whiplash. Again, I hoped the milk jug's forward ballast would minimize that.

Oh sure, there was also the possibility I'd capsize while riding the falls down. If I spun around like that, my helmeted head just might poke itself through that pretty water screen to slam on whatever rocks wanted to "play" me on the way to the pool. No, thanks. But I regarded that scenario as well down the list of possible disasters. Ensuring the vertical landing and keeping between the rock and the hard place—er, the flake and the shoulder—had my full attention.

Lilly

I worry a little bit, but if he happens to die kayaking, at least he was doing what he really, really wanted to do. I think it's great he is able to do something he absolutely loves, and is able to make way more money than me.

By that point in 1999, I'd been paddling very challenging whitewater full-time for six years—Class V and VI almost every day. No one had tutored me; I was self-taught because no one in my area wanted to kayak the stuff I was. I'd honed my instincts by trial and error, and my instincts had served me well. Like a businessman surrounded by an outstanding board of directors, I trusted my instincts implicitly. In my sport, things happen so fast that there often isn't time to think, only to react. So I've worked on turning my instincts into well-trained reactions.

Other people, viewing my youth and my predilection for what they considered suicidal whitewater, attributed my successes to luck and predicted my number would be up any day.

But I knew better because of my calculated approach and instincts. I believed then, as I believe now, that my instincts make the "yes I can" or "no I can't" decisions easy. I looked at Johnston that day and knew I could do it. It wasn't a decision made at a glance. I studied that falls for several hours before I said yes. After that, I was so busy visualizing how to thread that route and land vertically that my brain had zero room for doubt, fear, or further risk assessment. Which, when you think about it, is a good thing. I'd made up my mind, so now my entire focus was on the steps that I needed to take to run the falls successfully.

Dad

His activities are of significant concern, and I don't know any way to handle that other than to not think about it too much.

The observation deck became a mob scene as I walked my kayak to the same pool where we'd been shoving logs into the current. Cameras, arms, heads, bodies were jostling for the best position.

By then I had three trusted safety boaters waiting in their boats at the bottom pool, among them my best friend, Christian. Several other crew members were stationed to help if needed from land. And Eric and three other camera operators were fully positioned and ready. All that remained was to paddle to the selected slot on the falls' lip and push off. One way or another, I'd be at the bottom shortly.

Some paddlers used to throw their paddles away as they cruised over the lip to ensure that the paddle didn't end up hitting them in the teeth as they sank into the pool. I throw away my paddle only when it's a supereasy waterfall. In this instance, I wanted my paddle with me at the bottom in case the cave on the right intended to suck me in. Besides, if your boat starts to go off course on the trip down, a little paddle work during the descent can help control your boat angle. Not that I'd think consciously about movement required while in the air; it had to be all instincts at that speed.

The observation deck crowd went very quiet as I paddled slowly toward the lip. The milk jug felt both odd and reassuring in my bow. Like a form of resistance training, it forced me to put a little extra strength into my forward strokes. The current beneath my boat was slow all the way to the lip. I was 101 percent concentrated on disappearing over the lip at precisely the right point. I often take a paddle stroke on the way over the lip of a falls, but I didn't this time because I wanted to make sure that my bow dropped vertically.

I was free-falling, focusing, my mind and body on high alert. Normally, I tuck up—face against the deck of my boat—only just before hitting the water at the bottom, waiting to do so in case I need to be in position for some correction maneuver while falling (a twist of my hips, a jerk of my paddle). But when my left shoulder grazed that rock outcrop on the left, I instinctively tucked up, knowing I had just another fifteen feet until I hit the pool. Though I'd hoped to avoid it, that brush against the stone shoulder was far preferable to touching the midfalls flake, which would likely have pushed up my bow, milk jug or not.

The boils that sometimes form at the bottom of a waterfall are just what a kayaker wants. They soften the entry like a pillow. Well, okay, not quite like a pillow at the speed I was going. But compared with still water, a boil is a welcome feature. Falls without boils—even short falls without boils—require more caution, a different level of risk assessment.

Johnston's boils embraced and closed over me and my speeding boat as best they could. They let me penetrate deeply into the pool before aggressively slingshotting me back to the surface. But not before snapping my paddle in half on impact. My paddle was built to take 840 pounds of pressure, which gives you an idea of the force with which my boat and body slammed into the water.

I rolled up with half a paddle, a bruised shoulder, and a world record. And just like the test logs we'd pushed over the falls, I'd resurfaced free of the cave's sinister currents. My first sight was a welcome one: Christian's relieved face.

The shoulder wasn't a big deal; it was just a little sore from the glancing hit I took off the rock wall. I couldn't hear the gathering on the observation deck high above, but the crowd could see me and was roaring its approval.

Media response to this world record was much bigger than I expected. I'd paddled the waterfall to push the boundaries of what people considered possible, because that's what I love doing. But the media turned it into a bit of a spectacle. I was featured by *Dateline, Ripley's Believe it or Not!, Guinness World Records Primetime,* Fox, *Sports Illustrated,* and many other media outlets. Christian told one interviewer that it really defined what I had become, and I suppose he was right.

Was Johnston a particularly risky venture? Yes, in that no one could predict what the impact would do to my body. But just because it has stood as a world record for more than seven years doesn't mean it's the riskiest thing I've done. At least it was one straight shot; there was no risk of capsizing in a pool on the way down and being unable to roll up in time for the next plunge. Those types of falls are in some ways riskier.

Risk is relative, and as sports go, whitewater is less risky than most in terms of injuries—although not in terms of paying the ultimate price, death. Kayakers don't get injured as much as motocross racers, for instance. When motocross racers crash, they break bones. When kayakers crash—even when they crash big—it involves water, which is pretty forgiving. The most common injury in whitewater kayaking is dislocating a shoulder. Some paddlers have dislocated a shoulder so many times that they've learned to pop the shoulder back in under water before rolling back up.

Extreme kayakers have been known to break their ankles or a leg from hitting rocks under water after going over a waterfall. Others have broken their backs or ribs, or caught their faces on a rock. These things happen, but nowhere near as much as in sports such as motocross. In paddling, you're likely to either get away with it or drown. There's not a lot of middle ground between, but drownings are pretty rare. Drownings are most likely to happen when you go under a log or an undercut rock, or get recirculated in a hole (whirlpool) longer than you can hold your breath.

I know when I climb into my kayak that I can die doing what I do, but I'm not someone who is tolerating risk; I am deliberately seeking it out. That's how one pushes the envelope of a sport, how one challenges oneself. But let's be perfectly clear: I do not have a death wish. It's risk I'm seeking, not death. And it's years of knowledge and practice, and years of honing my instincts, that I believe help me paddle the fine line between them.

When I climb into my kayak, I don't feel fear or experience an adrenaline rush. I believe that fear and adrenaline stem from doubt, and I never doubt myself. Instead, I concentrate on my past kayaking successes to keep my mind positive. On the occasion when I make a mistake, I immediately visualize redoing it perfectly, to return my mind to thoughts of success. I do this because I believe that success comes from success. Once you are used to success, you don't accept anything less.

Not having fear allows me to be very good at what I do. That distinguishes me from people who allow fear to hold them back from attempting something. But my lack of fear also makes what I do more dangerous. It forces me to make decisions based purely on calculation; no emotion is involved. For me, that keeps it simple: a matter of risk relative to reward, not unlike the way an investor would approach a stock market purchase. It makes sense to invest in risky stock only if it offers a higher return.

In her book *The Romance of Risk: Why Teenagers Do the Things They Do,* Lynn E. Ponton says that adolescence is a time for risk taking and that it helps develop cognitive skills. She says, "Experimenting with new behaviors and feelings can promote more complex thinking, increase confidence, and help develop a young person's ability to assess and undertake risks in the future."

A Carnegie Institute study in 1995 suggested that American youths are "at greater risk today because they take more risks and are exposed to even more opportunities for dangerous risks than at any other time in American history."

I don't know about the latter—unless it means teens are rebelling against today's overprotective parents—but I'll go along with Ponton's vote that risk taking is a "normative, healthy, developmental behavior for adolescents."

Academics who like to put us risk takers under a microscope (or on a sofa), say that we tend to be extroverts with a high need for stimulation and novel sensations, that there's a connection between risk taking and testosterone, and that it peaks in late adolescence. Well, duh. And that we shy away from commitments in relationships. (Okay, I've already admitted that.) They've come up with cute names for us, including "sensation seekers" and "arousal seekers," and divided us into at least four types. The best type, of course, is TASers—as in "thrill and adventure seekers." Gosh, I feel so much better having a scientific name.

Academics, such as Marvin Zuckerman, who've built careers studying us tag high-risk sports as a "socially acceptable" outlet for sensation seekers who don't want to take on the risks of drugs or violence. Hey, sounds good to me. Keep us off the streets and on the rivers!

Grandma Doreen

I was really shocked when Tao started doing this kayaking. I've adapted to accepting what Tao does because I haven't got the emotional energy to stay worried.

In fact, parks and recreation staff often win funding for building rock-climbing walls, bungee-jumping towers, and the like—by citing studies that indicate at-risk youths who take up risky sports get in less trouble. Given my own narrow escape from the drug and fighting scene, I'm all for that. Kids don't need someone telling them not to do drugs; they need someone helping them find something positive on which to focus their energy. Once they have that, they lose the desire to go down a negative path.

So, have researchers come up with anything more useful than the above? Well, studies show that there are fewer female than male TASers (big surprise) but that the under-thirty female TASers are pretty hardcore. No problem, but those aren't the kinds of women I want to date. Which is kind of interesting, because, according to Zuckerman, opposites attract in the general population, but sensation seekers are an exception: they tend to go for each other, which he says suggests that risk taking has a "biological importance."

So there! But don't look for Tao Juniors anytime soon. I'm still very much a bachelor, and I like my lifestyle.

I tend to belittle or shrug off shrinks who think they know about risk taking or risk takers. My lack of interest in psychologists probably stems from the fact that my parents occasionally dragged us in to see one in hopes of ensuring that their split didn't have a negative effect on us. Pretty ironic to begin with, so I don't need to comment further on that. Suffice it to say those sessions were a waste of time.

But when I recently forced myself to page through an academic tome titled *Sensation Seeking and Risky Behavior* by that Zuckerman dude (American Psychological Association, 2006), a few comments caught my eye. Here they are:

- Risk depends on how you view it.

- The hedonistic rewards of sensation seeking are perceived as benefits only by high sensation seekers, [who] either underestimate the risks or are willing to accept them because the benefits are judged to outweigh them.

- The major source of fatalities are those endangering health, particularly smoking and drinking. . . . Students markedly underestimate annual fatalities due to smoking, drinking, and driving, and overestimate those due to risky sports.

Of course, if you're into psychobabble, you might like to take the following quiz, known as the ZKPQ analysis. (Stands for Zuckerman-Kuhlman Personality Questionnaire.) Then again, if you're reading this book, chances are you already know where you stand.

1. I often do things on impulse.

2. I would like to take off on a trip with no preplanned or definite routes or timetables.

3. I enjoy getting into new situations where you can't predict how things will turn out.

4. I sometimes like to do things that are a little frightening.

5. I'll try anything once.

6. I would like the kind of life where one is on the move and traveling a lot, with lots of change and excitement.

7. I sometimes do "crazy" things just for fun.

8. I prefer friends who are excitingly unpredictable.

9. I often get so carried away by new and exciting things and ideas that I never think of possible complications.

10. I like "wild," uninhibited parties.

Just for the record, I don't do wild, uninhibited parties—well, okay, maybe on occasion—but Zuckerman's got my number on half of these questions. So I guess I half-fit the definition of a TASer (thrill and adventure seeker) on Zuckerman's SSS (sensation seeking scale).

What no one has ever been able to tell me, however, is why I don't get butterflies in my stomach at the top of a horrendous drop. Sometimes even I find it scary that I don't really experience fear. Sometimes it bothers me, and I wonder if it's a minor chemical imbalance that makes me indifferent to risk. I don't really believe that's the case, but it's strange having a personality that I don't always understand. It's bizarre having no answers to questions about something that plays such a major role in what I'm doing with my life. It doesn't seem natural that I can paddle toward the lip of a falls knowing that the consequences of a mistake could include death, and feel indifferent to that.

As a very, very young child, I do remember being terrified of the aspens that swayed and creaked in the wind on a ridge I had to traverse alone and sometimes in the dark to meet a childhood friend who lived a mile away. I believed monsters lived among those trees. So perhaps my childhood forced me to grow up in a hurry where fear was concerned;

Osho

There are times I'm concerned about [the danger in what Tao does], but I accept it. He's going to do what makes him happy, and that's what I want him to do as well, so I suck it up. It's not like I wake up every day wondering if Tao is going to make it and I'm going to get the news. So I just choose not to think about it any more than I need to.

perhaps it forced me to deal with fear until I was no longer conscious of having it. These days, parents would never let a seven-year-old walk through trees and mountains in the dark. But I wouldn't change my childhood for anything. It molded me into who I am; it granted me confidence. It forced me to be creative, and it gave me the foundation for everything I'm doing today. That being said, I don't think my risk-taking personality is a product of my childhood; it's just who I am. Anyway, because I was pretty fearless as a child beyond the age of five, it took me half a lifetime to realize that I'm so unusual in not feeling fear. It wasn't until the media started paying attention to me and asking me how I deal with fear that I was forced to see myself as so very different from most people. It took me longer to realize that people are hard-pressed to accept my honest answer: that I simply don't feel fear. The only further explanation I can offer, which people find marginally more acceptable, is that my lack of fear stems from my high level of confidence — that, generally speaking, I believe I can pull off what I'm about to do.

A businessman will ask himself, "Do the risks outweigh the rewards?" Similarly, I ask myself, "What are the odds of being injured?" Some people use fear as a barometer of what they should and shouldn't do. Since I don't feel fear, I'm unable to use it to help me stay safe. That's not always a good thing. It means all the onus for staying safe is on my analytical skills. So I have to ask myself, again and again, "What are the chances I'll kill or hurt myself?"

Yes, sometimes I ponder why I'm such a risk taker. But such thoughts don't come to me the night before, or the minute before, I paddle over a waterfall. They come after I've put everything on the line. That's when I remind myself that I have a great life and that I don't need to risk it. That's when the logical side of myself says it doesn't make sense to risk my life to run a drop. But those are thoughts that come when I'm away from the river. When I'm at river's edge, something magnetic draws me to step into my kayak and prove I can do something. Every time I think I'm starting to mellow out, that magnetic force is all it takes to put me right back at the lip of a falls or rapid. Just as something compelled me to raise my fists when I was challenged as a child, I'm not easily able to walk away from a river that involves risk, especially if it involves pushing the limits of my sport.

Life would be boring without risk. Logically, it doesn't make sense that I'm risking my life just for the fun of it. But without fun, what is the purpose of life? I don't want to grow old and look back on my life wishing I'd done something that I chose not to do at the time because I was scared to take a chance. All successful people get their start by taking a chance.

My whole life has been an exploration of risk. As a kid jumping between trees, I always went for the tree farthest away that I thought I could land in. The risk of boredom is one of the reasons I keep running harder and harder stuff. When I'm out on a normal Class V run, I get bored pretty quickly. It's too easy. I have to take higher risks. I love knowing that I have to be perfect because the consequences of making a mistake are so severe. The only downside is, the longer I kayak and the better I get at it, the greater the level of risk I need to get the same level of focus.

Sometimes people ask me, "What about your family? Don't you think about them before you take big risks?" People don't understand that not only have I thought about this a lot, but that accordingly I actually hold myself back a bit in terms of what I choose to do. I have a great family, and I wouldn't want to put them through anything by dying in a kayaking accident. Especially when I was younger, I know I would have pushed things further if not for my concern about hurting my family members, in particular, my mom. I can't say that any of my three serious relationships with girlfriends have had the same effect; I experienced no holdback there.

I'm not as concerned about what happens to me as my family is; I just know that testing what can be done in a kayak is more important to me than worrying about the risk of dying. So having a family that really cares about me is what has kept me from pushing the limits too far and killing myself in the process.

THE RIGHT STUFF

*"Defining a big drop is almost as difficult as running one.
One man's terror is another's 'piece of cake.'"*

—Robert O. Collins and Roderick Nash,
The Big Drops: Ten Legendary Rapids

Sometimes, people ask, "Don't you worry about being a bad influence on younger kids?"

A bad influence on kids when too many kids these days aren't involved in any sports? A bad influence when I'm hired by schools to talk about goal-setting and staying free of drugs? Besides, the kids who are going to take a sport to the extreme are going to anyway. I'm not worried about kids taking risks in sports. There are far worse risks they could be taking.

Here are excerpts from a few of the fan letters I've received:

- "I would love if I could have the courage to face impending doom like you."

- "Just want to thank you for the inspiration in making it through life. I have had my challenges both mentally and physically, but your strong drive and ability to overcome something has shown me how to overcome fear in so many situations. I have learned through your determination that anything is possible, no matter how large a struggle life can be, so again, thank you."

- "What you do is incredible! The world needs crazy people like you. You are extraordinary."

- "Good on ya for your tenacity and good sense. Keep those big drops coming. You are an inspiration!"

And here's one from a four-year-old in Denver, Colorado. "You're cool. I saw you on TV going down a river. You're a cool kayaker. I like motorcycles. Do you like motorcycles or dinosaurs better?"

I always answer fan mail. I figure if they take the time to write me, I should find the time to respond. Besides, it means a lot to me that I can be a positive influence in someone's life.

A lot of kids these days are bored by team sports. They don't want to watch baseball and basketball. Extreme sports have a higher "cool factor"; extreme sports athletes have more color and passion. They also have more on the line, are more interesting to watch.

Anyway, if people never stretched their own abilities for fear of influencing others to go beyond their own skill levels, then nobody would be pushing forward in any field. Are race car drivers responsible for drivers who speed on the road? If a skateboarder does a 900, is he responsible for a kid who goes out and does a 900 before he's ready?

Ultimately, we need to be responsible for our own decisions. If I happened to be watching a crowd of kids viewing my extreme videos and clamoring about wanting to do whitewater for which they're not ready, I'd just tell them that paddling above their skill level is going to get them hurt. Paddlers learn early on that when on a river, they need to make all their decisions themselves, need to paddle what they feel is safely within their skill levels. Perhaps participants of individualistic sports such as whitewater kayaking internalize that before, and better than, members of team sports.

No, my influence on young people doesn't strike me as something to worry about. What does bug me is how many young paddlers hear the word *unrunnable* and don't question it, don't even consider attempting the whitewater so labeled. Needless to say, I was always someone who questioned such a description. I like to question everything; I ask "why" before conforming to the consensus. I've often found that if I believe something is possible, there is a way.

For many years, people considered Class V the top of the scale: the hardest level of navigable whitewater. Then more and more paddlers began accepting that Class VI sections were being run, and the scale was altered to include that category. But the stuff that I and a number of other paddlers are running these days is unquestionably more than Class VI. That means that Class VII is being kayaked, and the official scale should be Class I through VII. Of course, people resist change, and I think that the lack of consensus to include VII is an example of people resisting change for the sake of resisting change.

So what does it take to be an extreme kayaker? Half of being a good kayaker is mental. By that I mean it doesn't matter how physically talented you are or how great your fitness level is; if you can't handle the risks that go along with it, you'll never be successful as an extreme kayaker. You're putting a lot on the line. You have to be able to cope mentally with the dangers.

You need to be in good shape, because sometimes you take a lot of impact even when you do things right. But that's just part of the equation. I'd liken it to investing in the stock market. If you're not a risk taker, you'll put more in bonds than stocks. If you're not a risk taker, it doesn't matter how much skill you have; you will always paddle whitewater below that of which you are capable. There is nothing wrong with that. Pushing the limits isn't for everyone.

Sometimes I see kayakers with incredible skill who can never paddle to their physical limits because they don't have the right frame of mind. Their fears hold them back. Those fears keep them safe, but also keep them from taking the sport as far as they otherwise could. I could say the same thing about people and careers. Most people don't do as well as they could because it takes guts—confidence in their abilities—as well as skill to give up their salaries and create something bigger and better. I've chosen to go for it in my sport, but all of us deal with the same types of issues in life. It's a matter of looking at risks and deciding if we're comfortable taking them.

My return on the risks I'm willing to take is personal; I do it for the feeling of personal achievement. Now that I've got a niche in the industry and sponsors with expectations, some people assume that I need to take bigger and bigger risks to continue to please the sponsors. They don't understand that with me, it works the opposite way. I've always had expectations I put on myself. I answer to these above all. These days, if I make a mistake, I have more to lose. For instance, ten years ago, if I busted an ankle, no one knew or cared; it wasn't a big deal. It'd be a bummer, but that would be all. I wouldn't get bad press.

Christian Knight

Tao finds qualities in people that he really admires and then adopts that.

Today, if I were to get seriously injured, I could lose contracts and money; I could lose sponsors. So from many standpoints, including financial, it would make sense for me to lower some risks. But that makes sense only to those who don't know me. There's a reason I've been so careful with financial planning that I can now drop the sport when I want to. I have a good financial cushion now, one that would allow me to live for many years with dropped sponsors or an injury demanding time for recovery.

So I can ignore the pressure that would influence other individuals to change their ways. I can stay true to myself, paddling for the reasons I've always paddled—to push back the frontiers of my chosen sport and

to fulfill my own inner drive to respond to challenges as they arise. The money, the sponsors, the reputation are all just a vehicle to allow me to do this. They never have been and never will be the driving force. They will never be my main influence, let alone enslave me.

Here's an example: Two years ago I went to Mexico to run a hundred-foot-plus cascading waterfall for a Discovery Channel television show. I chose to do this when the water and weather were optimal. It was abysmally nonproductive in terms of my sponsorship contracts, which all came up for renewal the following month. Imagine if I'd injured myself on the Mexican falls. I might well have suffered sponsors walking away from me. The more prudent decision would have been to delay that run until my contracts were signed and my ongoing salary assured.

Businesspeople would shake their heads at my foolishness, but I'm a kayaker before I'm a businessman. I really, really wanted to run that drop. Why? Because I'm risk driven. Anyway, I believed very strongly that I could run that falls successfully, without injury.

As corny as it may sound, this goes straight back to my childhood. My mother always taught us to believe in ourselves and if we wanted to do something, to go for it. It was a great way to prepare us for the real world. Ironically, however, as soon as I started to take major risks in my kayak, my mom started singing a different tune. My parents weren't too supportive for a long time. My father probably respects the business approach I've taken. But I don't think he respects some of the stuff I've done in my kayak. Same goes for my grandparents. Nobody seemed able to approve of what I was doing until my activities showed up on the evening news.

I've always courted risk. I love risk. I thrive on it. When I was eighteen, I decided with a couple of friends that I was going to climb Mount

Shasta in California. The fact that I'd never gone mountaineering in my life was no deterrent. And just to ensure it'd be an adventure, we decided against tackling the usual route, opting instead for a less popular route on the south side of the mountain. Shasta is around fourteen thousand feet in elevation. We made our way to the ten thousand-foot mark and set up camp. Two of us decided to try to summit the next day. Rising early the next morning, we hiked until the going got pretty steep. At this point, we were faced with two options: We could take a relatively direct route straight up to the summit. Or we could take an easier, more indirect route that wound around the mountain before reaching the top. I wanted to take the more challenging, direct route, but my companion was pushing for the indirect one. So we decided to split up and see who reached the summit first. After my buddy left, I dug out my ice ax and crampons. I'd never used these before, but it all seemed pretty straightforward to me: you slam the ice ax in, start kicking steps into the snow, and make your way up. After doing this for what seemed like hours, I looked down to gauge my progress. My eyes narrowed to see an enormous crevasse no more than five hundred feet below me. I had no ropes and no training in the sport, but I knew I'd better be careful not to tumble backward into that gap. *Just keep going up,* I told myself.

As I approached the top, I sensed that the altitude was making everything more difficult. Plus, wind gusts were now howling over the summit, occasionally catching my backpack as if determined to pluck me off the face and send me reeling backward. I estimated those winds at about fifty miles per hour.

I was tiring, and I craved a break, but because I wasn't roped up to anything or anyone, I dared not rest anywhere exposed to that wind.

Instead, I made my way across an icy slope to a rock outcrop and clung to it, trying to regain enough energy for a final attack on the summit.

This is dumb, I told myself. *Why am I always getting myself into these situations?*

Then I turned my attention back to the mountain, kicking steps into the hard snow and ice. Two to three hours from the time my friend and I had parted, I found myself on the summit amid a throng of people who'd come up on the main route.

Just great, I mused. *I do all this work to get somewhere tranquil, and it's a mob scene. Oh well.*

I sat and waited about two hours, shifting and shivering to stay warm, until my friend showed up. We laughed and drank from our canteens, then hightailed it back to base camp. Such adventures make for great memories that I can treasure for life.

Another time I tend to court danger is when rivers go into flood. That's actually my favorite time to paddle. Once in 2002, water on the Skykomish River in Washington was rising so fast that people were warned to vacate their homes. That's when my buddies and I loaded our boats and hurried to the river's edge. We got there about the time water started flowing into those homes. Old-growth trees along the riverbank were falling into the current with terrific splashes. Rumor had it that the river was going to hit one hundred thousand cubic feet per second. That's more than ten times its normal flow of eight thousand. On the river, I was eddied out behind a log at one point when I looked upstream to see an old-growth log powering toward me. It was about four feet thick and one hundred fifty feet long—definitely not your average log. I shot out of that eddy, and just in time. The old-growth tree slammed into the smaller log so hard that it took the little log out, ushering it downstream. A while later, I was surfing a thirty-foot wave when big logs came shooting out of the water like bullets and landing all around me. I looked toward shore and saw someone in his driveway loading all his furniture into a U-Haul. Within an hour, all the houses along the river were covered with water. Meanwhile, we were having the time of our lives.

Osho

I think Tao has fear but perceives it differently than most people. He is less deterred by it—especially if someone says something is not possible.

When you live life on the edge, you really have to be flexible. I learned that on a trip to the Dominican Republic, where we were shooting a video. Josh Bechtel, Eric Link, a guy named Tyko Isaacson, and I had arranged for some people to hike our gear to a point in a canyon where we'd meet them while doing a first descent. We hadn't counted on it raining so hard that our helpers wouldn't be able to get to us. Tropical rain can come in torrential downpours, and the hikers were unable to cross a certain creek to bring us our food and bedding. As the four of us came off the river, we knew we had only rescue gear, a first-aid kit, and three bivvy sacks among us. Grudgingly, Josh and I decided to share a bivvy sack that night. But just getting into it turned out to be a challenge. Josh, being skinnier than I was, stepped into it first, standing up. Then I stepped in, we drew it up around us, and we agreed to fall to the ground because the bag was too tight around us to allow us to bend our knees. One, two, three, "timber." Okay, we were now lying in it, but to get out of the wind, we needed to roll it into a nearby ditch, where Eric and Tyko were sitting and laughing at us. Oops; we were now in the ditch, but we'd stretched the seams so much that water was entering through them. In the meantime, the rain picked up. After a while, we found the ditch filling with water. And there we were, lying in two inches of water in a bivvy sack full of holes.

In winter in the Dominican Republic, it can stay dark a very long time. For twelve long hours, while Tyko and Eric slept, Josh and I lay in that ditch telling jokes. Many people would look back on an experience like that as one of the worst nights of their lives. But to me, times like that make for fun memories. Not fun at the time, but the best of memories.

Of course, when you take on risks, things can go wrong. Once, on a trip in Argentina, I decided to run a hundred-foot, two-tiered, sliding waterfall where water from the second tier landed on a rock ledge. It fed into a giant lake, which we'd crossed by motorboat. I decided to run the falls in the middle even though it had two little granite kickers on its first tier. I knew that each of those kickers would launch me upward, but I figured I could still keep things under control.

Unfortunately, I landed on the rock ledge below the first kicker with so much force that it slammed my body rag-doll-style off to one side of the boat, which put me off balance. As I struggled to quickly lift my chest back up, I hit the second kicker, which shot me ten feet into the air and turned me upside down. I was now headed toward the rock I'd intended to land on—but I was approaching it headfirst at about twenty-five miles per hour. I barely managed to bring my hands over my face in time. Smash! I did a face-plant on the rock, my ribs also taking much of the impact. I rolled up immediately so that I wouldn't continue sliding down the falls on my face, chest, and hands, and then I slid the rest of the way into the safety of the lake. I knew before my kayak bobbed to a stop that I was hurt badly. I was convinced I had a rib sticking right out of my chest and into my life jacket. It hurt so badly that I refused to take off my life jacket, believing that it might be better to let it hold the rib in place. I also had scraped knuckles, and blood was dripping from a small cut near my eye.

There was no medical crew on this particular trip, just four friends and myself somewhere in the middle of Argentina. We'd ridden several miles across the lake by Zodiac, and the only sensible plan was to motor back across the expansive lake to where I could get checked out at a hospital. When the boat ran out of gas midlake, my four able-bodied companions started paddling. I didn't offer to help, because I was in too much pain.

It wasn't long before my friends got bored, so they were pleased when someone produced a bottle of whiskey. They passed it around between stretches of paddling as I sat there forcing a smile. Pretty soon they were so drunk that one of them fell into the lake, which pitched the other three into gales of laughter. I tried hard not to laugh, because it put me in agonizing pain. But it was kind of funny. Here I was, stranded on a lake at the mercy of four very wasted friends who seemed to have forgotten that I was in torment.

It took about three hours to reach shore and get ourselves into a town. At the town's hospital, I gritted my teeth as one of my drunk friends eased off my life jacket and dry top. No protruding bone. That was one good thing. The hospital X-rayed me and informed me that I had not broken my ribs; I'd only torn my oblique muscles. I was back in my kayak within nine days.

Christian Knight

I wouldn't be able to comment on Tao's pain tolerance because he hasn't been hurt much. I know, though, that he'll never admit when he's sick. He'll say he's "fighting something off." He always looks at matters in the most optimistic terms. In Guatemala once, he drank water he thought was drinking water. But it was river water. He started puking, and then as soon as he felt better, he said, "Well, I'm back to being Berman." But half an hour later, he started puking again. Overall, he's got really good health, and he doesn't seem to get injured, maybe because he's small and compact and has good instincts. I've known him fifteen years and never really seen him hurt.

Looking back on that crash, I tried to determine what had gone wrong and what I could do to prevent a similar outcome in the future. I realized that I had underestimated the waterfall; my complacency was to blame.

Any time I can get my friends hired for shoots, I try to do so, both because I trust them more than anyone else as safety crew and because it's fun to have them along. But this nearly backfired on me during a

Mexico in 2007. That's when Nate, a friend of a drop with a rescue throw-bag, got all his kayak when he realized he'd forgot- because there wasn't enough time to hike re with absolutely no safety equipment ine. Luckily for him and me, nothing went wrong!

Another time, I was the one who learned about preparedness the hard way. I was in Chile on the second day of a shoot when someone tossed a boat over a fence. It landed on and cracked my helmet, which was lying on the ground. With no backup helmet, I was forced to apply duct tape, Super Glue, and chicken wire to hold that helmet together for the next two weeks of being filmed on difficult whitewater. After that, I made sure I brought extras of every piece of equipment.

Of course, no amount of preparation can guarantee that things will go smoothly. Once, when several of us were running a river as training for a race, my buddy Tyko started down a steep section. Positioned in my kayak below the drop, I remember sitting bolt upright as I saw his kayak

Jock Bradley

I admire Tao for what he is able to do in a kayak. Very few people can do it as well as he can. If he tells me he's going to paddle something that to my eye looks absolutely impossible, I trust that he can, and then he does it safely. From a working perspective, that's imperative to me. I work with my friends, and I don't want to see anyone get hurt.

stop abruptly. Even before I could leap out and grab my rescue rope, I knew that Tyko's boat was stuck—pinned—halfway down the drop.

As I ran toward him, I saw that a terrific volume of water was pouring onto his rock-trapped plastic boat. This was applying such pressure that the boat was folding onto his legs, which I knew would make it impossible for him to get himself out or for any of us to pull him out. With some difficulty, I reached Tyko and tied my rescue rope to his bow, then tossed the rope to my companions and shouted at them to start pulling on it from various angles. It was the type of situation in which an elaborate procedure called a Z-drag might have worked, but we knew there was no time to set that up.

Within a minute, the river water in the pocket of rocks where Tyko was stuck had risen to his shoulders. We knew we had two minutes maximum to extract him from his kayak or his kayak from the rocks. Frantically, we were setting up all kinds of rescue systems. As we worked, I had a sense of being in a horror movie, seeing the way the water crept up Tyko's neck, then over his nose.

We eventually determined that the best angle from which we needed to pull required one of us to position himself directly downstream. So I held onto the rope and jumped into the current, hoping my body weight would pull his boat free. Tyko was now completely submerged, and my action failed to dislodge his boat. Bechtel realized that my weight in the current wasn't enough, so he grabbed my rope and jumped into the current, too. All of a sudden, we felt the rope go slack. Did that mean that the rope had broken or that we'd managed to dislodge the boat's bow? Five seconds later, we had our answer: Tyko's boat—totally bent out of shape—slid to the bottom of the drop, and Tyko emerged from it, a hand raised to show us he was alive and well. No more than thirty seconds could have elapsed from the time the water had risen over Tyko's face to the time he and his boat had popped up. But it had been an excruciatingly long thirty seconds. The situation was one of the sketchiest I'd seen—like watching a movie in fast-forward.

Still, I don't view anything as a mistake as long as it doesn't kill anyone and I don't make the error twice.

Another humbling experience involved a river run near Mount Rainier with a ten-foot drop into a very swirly section of water that then plunged another forty feet. It didn't look all that difficult, so I didn't scout it for long. I shot over the first ledge, but before I could take on the second portion of the falls, the water shoved me hard into the eddy with strong, swirling currents. For thirty minutes, I tried and tried to punch through the current to get to the falls' second lip, but the current was having none of it. I was upright and stable, but trapped. Eventually, members of my party had to rappel down a cliff to reach me. With their rope's help, my boat and I managed to get up the wall and out of there.

I'm usually the one who performs rescues with fellow paddlers, and it was very humbling to require one myself. But the fact is, I could not have gotten out without help.

Rescuing others can be as challenging and dangerous as keeping oneself alive. Whenever I scout a river section I'm about to tackle, I'm not just calculating where I intend to go. I'm scanning it for where someone else might end up—where a friend might find himself in a dangerous situation. I'm looking for the hazard and thinking about what could happen well before anyone puts paddle to water. After I've done my run, I deliberately place myself as close to that danger as possible. That way, if someone ends up there, I'm immediately on hand to help. People often think it's a coincidence that I'm often the first to reach a pinned paddler. Few realize it's premeditated. My reaction when things go wrong may appear casual to some, but for me, this type of crisis is a frequent occurrence.

One of my most harrowing rescue experiences was retrieving a friend named Walter from an undercut rock. We'd paused above a Class V rapid, where I'd figured out the best line to take. I explained it to Walter, agreed to let him run the rapid first, and asked him to wait at the bottom of the rapid for the rest of us.

Christian Knight

I definitely think Tao has fear. Everyone has fear. He just manages it better than anyone I know. I've seen him look scared and act scared, but not scared in a way that would arrest his logic or physical abilities.

I then advised the others how to run the rapid and entered the current myself. When I neared the bottom of the rapid, I realized that Walter wasn't where he should be. I looked about just in time to see the top of his helmet appear briefly between the river's surging waterline and a large, flat rock that protruded from shore. Then it disappeared again in the water gurgling beneath that "roof" of a stone slab.

He's stuck beneath an undercut rock, I thought grimly, and I paddled as fast as I could for that rock. By the time I reached it, I had seen his helmet resurface three or four times, always disappearing beneath the surface again. I could tell there wasn't enough space between the water's surface and the underside of the rock for his face to bob up to where he could catch a quick breath before the current yanked him under water again. I could only see the top of his yellow helmet banging against the overhanging rock, so I knew there wasn't much time.

I landed just upstream of the scene, jumped out of my boat, and lay full-length on my stomach atop the rock.

The next time his head bobbed up, I shoved my arms as deeply as they'd go into the water and grabbed his life jacket. Muscles straining, fully determined, I hauled him out and over onto the top of that rock. He gasped and heaved and finally gathered sufficient breath to tell his story. Once he'd become trapped under the rock, he'd come out of his kayak. For the past forty-five seconds, he'd been using his feet to push off the bottom of the river in an unsuccessful attempt to get himself to the surface for air. Had I reached him any later, he'd have drowned. Walter's kayak, of course, had long since gone on downstream. We retrieved it later.

As I've said before, undercut rocks are one of the most dangerous of all river features. Among my own many close calls, the nearest I've come to dying (not counting the crane incident when I was a teen) involved an undercut rock—ironically, on a Class II river. I paddled up to a rock to "splat" on it, a trick in which the paddler briefly lays his boat perpendicularly against a river object, then paddles off it.

The second I hit this particular rock, I realized that it was undercut. Instead of glancing off it, I found my boat getting sucked under it. Then my boat stopped, as stuck onto that rock as if it had been glued. I was about two feet under water, pinned on that rock. There was so much force from the water that I couldn't move, and my boat wasn't going anywhere either. My thoughts were, "So this is what it feels like to be pinned on a rock under water. Am I really going to die on a Class II? How silly and ironic if I die here on such an easy piece of whitewater."

I didn't panic. I had this strange, relaxing sensation, as if I were lying on a sofa watching a grim situation unfold on television in front of me. I wish I could say that it bothered me more, but it didn't. I just had this detached curiosity about whether I was going to live or not.

I should try to get out of my kayak, I thought. I pulled my spray deck off and started fighting to pull myself out of the boat. I got most of the way out, but one leg wouldn't budge. It was twisted into an awkward position, and the force of the water was threatening to break it off at the knee.

With all the concentration I'd used to climb halfway out of the boat, I managed to climb back in, straighten that leg, and climb out again. I was now under water, pinned against my kayak, still unable to breathe. I was having a difficult time telling up from down, so I searched for what might be sunlight and pushed toward it. Next thing I knew, I was being dragged and tumbled by the current, and, after about five seconds, allowed to the surface to breathe. It was another minute before the undercut rock released my boat.

Afterward, I remember sitting on a rock in the sun, reflecting on what had just occurred. It was a reminder to never get complacent on any river, as well as a reminder that the line between a safe route and a complete disaster can be less than half a foot. I was pleased that I hadn't panicked. I'd been calm, analytical. And yet, as I stared at the rock that had nearly done me in, I couldn't help feeling that the experience had been kind of fun, too. No doubt that sounds like I don't care what happens to me, but I do. I have a great life, great friends and family. But for some damn reason, I just love flirting with death.

Risk is something I've embraced as a lifestyle. It's something I take on every day. Besides keeping my instincts sharp, it expands my sense of humor.

Once, Eric Link, five other paddlers, and I and were doing a first descent of a river in Canada when we came to a horizon line.

This looks like a huge waterfall, I thought. *And there's only one eddy close enough to the lip to allow us to scout from our boats.* I pointed to it and made sure everyone heard me: "We have to catch that eddy!"

I went first. As I swung into the eddy, a dull thunder filled my ears and spray shot up from down below, rising to just behind my boat's tail. That waterfall sounded massive.

I turned my head back upriver, only to see my companion Chris trying frantically to catch the eddy I was in. He was treading water with his paddle, his tail about to be sucked over the lip. He went wide-eyed just before the water sucked him over the ledge. He'd missed the eddy!

Eric cruised neatly into the eddy and looked about. "Where's Chris?" he asked, his eyes narrowing.

"He went over the falls."

"No way!" Eric looked as horrified as I felt.

We still couldn't tell from our eddy how tall the falls was and what lay at the bottom of its pour-over. So without exchanging another word, we paddled our boats to shore, sprang out, and pulled out our rescue ropes. We stepped cautiously to where we could peer over the edge.

My chest relaxed. It was only a thirty-five-footer, and there was Chris, still in his kayak but without his paddle, clinging to a rock wall. The entire river was pulsing beneath Chris's boat, up and down two feet at a time. From where Chris was struggling to stay put, he couldn't see what was around the corner, but we could. Judging from the tense face that looked up at us, he was assuming the worst: maybe another giant drop filled with logs, followed by a man-swallowing whirlpool hole. In fact, however, the river turned the corner and went completely placid.

Eric and I just looked at each other and burst out laughing.

Chris peered up at us with terror on his face. But from our expressions, he clearly realized it must be safe, so he released his grip on the wall and let the water take him to where his paddle was waiting.

When you're in my line of work, you see dicey situations so often that for some reason, you just start to see humor in them. If you court risk for a living, you might as well see the humor in some of the situations. How else would living on the edge be fun and worthwhile?

PRIMED

"The conditions of conquest are always easy.
We have but to toil awhile, endure awhile, believe always,
and never turn back."

—Seneca the Elder,
Roman rhetorician and writer

We were high in the Austrian Alps, in a charming village not far from Mozart's birthplace. She was young and cute and had a bubbly personality. So I was more than willing to let the young lady in the white lab coat examine me.

Clipboard in hand, she led me to a consultation room in the state-of-the-art Red Bull training center, where elite athletes from around the world fly in to train. I was wearing nothing but shorts. She motioned me to a bench.

"So," she said, placing her fingers on my wrist and casting her eyes on her watch, "the stationary bike got your heart rate up."

"Sure did," I said, giving her my most winning grin.

"Next I want to examine each part of your body that has been injured."

"Sure," I said, shifting my bare feet on the gleaming stone floor, fully prepared to offer her whatever demonstration of athletic prowess she fancied. "Only trouble is, I don't have any injuries."

She laughed. A polite, professional laugh.

"I'm being honest," I said, amused that a physiotherapist who specializes in athletes thought I was giving her a hard time.

Her eyes narrowed, just a little, and she tapped a pencil on her clipboard. "Most athletes," she informed me patiently, "have lots of injuries, enough to fill up a page."

"Okay," I relented, "I fell off a crane when I was a kid and had no heartbeat for about forty-five seconds. I had to be resuscitated. And as a child, I broke both arms at different times, and a couple of fingers. But I've never had a serious injury. In fact, I've never had a serious injury since I started kayaking."

Lilly

When they were teenagers, Tao and Osho had a
pull-up bar at Mom's house. They used to see who
could do the most or run the fastest. They were
very competitive.

"Never an injury from kayaking?"

"Well, once I landed sort of upside down on a rock when I was kayaking over a waterfall. That made me limp for a week. And once I scraped
up my shoulder. But those weren't really injuries."

"I see," she said, scribbling on her paper, her eyes roving over my
body.

She measured the spaces between my vertebrae to make sure that
all the impacts I'd had over the years hadn't added up to a crushing effect.

"Put your arms out to your side, then lift them above your head."

I tried, but could raise them no higher than to a horizontal position
at shoulder height. That had been true for as long as I could remember; I'd
never worried about it.

"Come on, no messing with me," she teased.

"Can't raise them any higher," I told her. "Honest. I can't remember
the last time I was able to."

Her eyebrows rose, and her hands reached out to touch my arms.
"I've never seen this before. We may have a serious issue here." But after

Rolling this rock is part of my training.

calling in some colleagues and questioning me some more, she was able to reassure me.

"You've so overdeveloped your back muscles from all the time you spend in your boat that they're getting in the way of your shoulder blades being able to rotate. You have muscle overhanging the bone pivots. That's why you can raise your arms forward and up, but not over your head from a horizontal position." She shook her head, whether in admiration or amusement, I wasn't sure. "If that works for you in kayaking, there's no need for us to suggest something different. Very interesting," she said, making me feel like either a bit of a mutant or a very special specimen— I wasn't sure which.

"Sounds good. I always thought it was just lack of flexibility."

"Nope. Not a flexibility issue."

Over the next few days, I was put through a battery of tests. Staff took blood out of my ear every five minutes to determine the lactic acid in my muscles. I spent time on a training bike. Once, as the lady physio to whom I'd been assigned was explaining something to me, Formula 1 racer Scott Speed wandered by in the hallway and gave me a quick smile and wave. He was one of the athletes I got to know during my week at the training center.

"As I was saying," my physio continued, "our goal is to determine what you're doing in your sport that might create long-term problems with your body."

She walked me over to an instrument that had pedals you turned with your arms while sitting down. I caught the word *biometrics* as she talked at me.

"...determine how long you can keep up the exercise as it gradually offers you more and more resistance."

"How long I can keep it up?" My ears perked up. "What's the longest anyone has ever managed to stay on it?"

With a hint of a smile, she told me.

"Okay, that's the time to beat. Let's do it," I said.

She was right about the machine being programmed to introduce more and more resistance. After a few minutes, I felt as if I was spinning something that needed serious oiling. My chest was heaving and my muscles were screaming.

The last few seconds I could barely continue, but I funneled most of my senses into watching the clock. I just had to beat that time, had to beat every athlete who'd ever stepped up to this pain machine.

The second hand on the clock moved as slowly as agony, but I was still on the machine, still pumping my juiceless arms with sweat pouring off my face. The very microsecond I knew I'd beaten that record, I died. At least, my arms died. I couldn't move them at all. I'd given it every last piece of energy I had.

I've no idea if I impressed my physio, but here's what was going through my mind: why did I have only enough strength to beat the record, and not one bit more? If the record had been just thirty seconds longer, I'm dead sure I'd have had thirty seconds more in me. Somehow, my body would've found the power to do it. I marveled at the mind–body connection I'd just demonstrated, at the proof that confidence plays such a key role in success.

As my physio walked me to the shrink's office, I wondered if she saw my secret scowl. *Great. Some twit is going to lay me on a sofa and pretend to read my mind. Shrinks are not my favorite kinds of people,* I reflected. I'd been enough times as a kid because of my parents' issues. But if Red Bull wanted me to see a sports psychologist as part of my routine here, whatever.

He sat me down at a desk with a computer. A program on the screen asked me endless questions, trying hard to reach into my psyche. I breathed a sigh of relief when I'd finally finished typing my answers.

The psychologist looked at my answers and smiled. "So, like many athletes, you have commitment issues."

That forced me to give the program a little more respect.

"And you have an analytical mind," he added.

He rambled on; those are the only two things he said that I remember. I was just very glad to get out of there.

As scientific as that Red Bull Center training was, I was surprised at the one area it didn't cover: nutrition and diet. I'm far from a gourmet cook, but I know how to eat nutritiously. When I was a child, I worked two to three hours every day in my mom's garden. It was our main source

Eric Link

I've videotaped a lot of kayakers, and Tao is a unique bird, for sure. He's so into challenges it's unbelievable. If you want to manipulate Tao, you just present something as a challenge. Even if he saw it as a trick, he'd do it because he's so compelled to take on and beat challenges. He comes up with ridiculous things for himself all the time: "I'm going to run up this mountain in fifteen minutes. If I lose, I have to drink this jug of maple syrup." Once, he ran up to tree line on a mountain in Cashmere, Washington. The guy who lost to him had to down a bottle of Mrs. Butterworth's syrup and immediately puked afterwards! Tao is the most into challenges of anyone I've ever seen. Nowadays he's pushing himself in multisport and running; he's totally into seeing what his body can do.

of food, sometimes supplemented by a chicken and the staples she shopped for every three months: oats, flour, wheat, and lentils. We ate very well. At my dad's, we weren't allowed to put sugar on the cornmeal we always had for breakfast; honey was healthier. I don't think either of my parents even kept sugar, and candy was certainly never allowed.

When I first moved down our mountain, somebody dragged me to fast-food places. The food there tasted terrible to me, and I knew it was unhealthy. I figure everyone who doesn't eat fast food has an advantage on his competitors, and I'm thankful that my upbringing never made it tempting.

Training on my road bike

These days, I'm not as serious about my diet as, say, a Tour de France rider, but I kick off every morning with four eggs and either whole-wheat toast, Grape-Nuts or hash browns. For lunch I typically eat leftover pasta, and for supper, salmon or other seafood or meat with pasta. When I'm training superhard, I'll put protein powder in drinks because otherwise I can't get enough protein through eating.

I drink lots of water all day long and chug the occasional sports drink. I don't measure my water or protein or carbs; I just know that the more I train, the more I need of them. I also eat a lot of fresh carrots to get enzymes. I like fish houses and pasta places, and spend a lot of evenings at the best Mexican and Thai eateries in my hometown. I don't enjoy going to fine restaurants where it costs hundreds of dollars to walk away hungry. As for all-you-can-eat restaurants, they typically use cheap ingredients and too much butter.

I don't really enjoy cooking, but I'm a decent cook, especially if the occasion involves a barbecue, and especially if I've got a female to impress.

For me, the most important aspect of training is staying motivated. Everyone has to figure out what works for him or her in that regard. Sometimes I picture competitors training that same morning, and I work to surpass whatever I imagine them doing. I'll do anything to stay motivated. The difference between great and just decent athletes is their level of commitment to training. People often talk about wanting to win, but not many actually put in the necessary training time to pull it off. My pain during training—and I'll detail my training in a moment—is the price I'm willing to pay to win.

Music helps. I listen to the radio, anything but jazz. As for weather, it doesn't matter what it's doing. If it's time to train, I train.

Scott Zagarino,

friend and managing director of Athletes for a Cure,
a fund-raising and awareness program of the Prostate
Cancer Foundation:

Tao is one of a kind. Tao and I met two years ago, when
I moved to Hood River. We were introduced by a mutual
friend and found ourselves kindred spirits immediately;
we both have way too much energy for our own good.

Tao is just one of those people who lives all out all the
time, like there isn't any tomorrow. He's interested in
everything. He's like a little kid that way. He's not an
adrenaline junkie so much as that rare type of person
who just wants to see if a problem can be solved. I love
that about him. He'll look at anything and try to figure
out if it can be done. He'll worry it like a dog with a bone

One cloudless summer day, I was riding my bike on a path along the
Columbia River when I spotted a river barge a mile ahead. *I'm going to catch*
that barge, I told myself, since I'm always looking for creative opportunities
to keep myself training. That barge was moving, but once I'd spotted it, so
was I. I cranked for a full hour, my eyes on that fat barge except when a train

till he can figure it out. That's what sets him apart from most other kayakers. That, and putting in the training time. His body is a tool that he keeps sharp. He's very respectful of that fact. He has a genetic gift, too—a huge genetic gift.

I manage sports programs for cancer research and have a long history in athletics. I'm as interested in training as Tao is in kayaking. There's a workout program called CrossFit (explained at www.crossfit.com) that I always put athletes through the first time we begin working together. I've seen hundreds of people use it, but I had never seen a person get through it the first time without stopping before I met Tao. The day I watched him do it for the first time, the other athletes in the room were pausing to throw up at intervals. Tao did thirty-six rounds, which is more rounds than anyone I've ever seen has done the first time.

sitting still on the tracks between us obscured my view. *Hey,* I thought as I neared the barge, *that train is going to start up any time. Then I'll race it, too.*

Sure enough, as I finally passed the barge, the train began rumbling behind me. *Well, I'll stay ahead of it as long as I can,* I decided, pouring myself into a new sprint. It takes a while for a train to accelerate, so despite

Scott Zagarino *(continued)*

A guy named Greg Glassman spent eighteen years developing CrossFit. It's the most comprehensive and punishing program there is for athletes. It values overall fitness. Thousands of laypeople do it, but it's mostly for athletes. It's exclusively what the most fit people on the planet use. Most people consider triathletes ultrafit, but they can't jump out of the way of a moving car without tearing a ligament. There's not much range of motion or strength required for being a triathlete. A boxer, on the other hand, has to move in all directions with power and draw on aerobic capacity for long periods of time and maintain an ability to power really hard and recover quickly to do it all over again. Those are the elements of fitness.

the windless day and ninety-degree-Fahrenheit heat, I was doing okay until I came to a hill. As fast as I pumped at that point, the train (now going thirty miles per hour) began to pass me—until I crested the hill and had gravity briefly on my side. By the time the train whistled past and I let myself ease up, I'd done a hard three-hour ride. I know this is kind of silly, but staying motivated is sometimes the hardest part of training. So I'm always looking for things to keep me motivated.

CrossFit measures strength, flexibility, and an ability to generate power or force with accuracy. It pays huge dividends for accuracy, which is not usually considered an element of fitness. But if you think about kayaking or wrestling, the ability to put all your power in your spot at one time is important. In other words, when Tao puts his paddle in the water, he puts it in with maximum force exactly where he wants it. A person who is fit in only one specific area can't do that.

There are three things that make Tao a successful athlete: a willingness to go for it, his volume of training, and his genetic gift. A lot of an athlete's ability hinges on genetics. You need a huge tolerance for discomfort. Tao and I train

While filming for the kayak video *Pulse,* some friends and I headed out one night to paddle a mile of Class V river with a twenty-five-foot waterfall. We shone our flashlights on the falls' lip to determine where to put in our last paddle strokes and push out. Then, as I headed over the lip, a photographer who came along started taking flash photos. All I could see were stars as I fell. I landed on my side, but it was okay because it was so dark that nobody could see my crash. The challenge made for a really fun night.

Scott Zagarino *(continued)*

together when whatever we're doing is synched up.
There aren't a lot of people training at Tao's level, period.
No kayakers that I know of.

He has definitely become a friend. I'm fifty, and I've probably
met three people in my life I'd compare to Tao in terms of
absolutely going for it every minute. He doesn't just throw
himself at things. It's half mind and half body. For instance,
he's much better versed on personal finance than most
people I know because he was interested in knowing about it.

My best friend is a Marine Corps captain, an athlete, a poet,
and someone who graduated from an elite music program with
honors. Tao is the only person I know who compares

Cross-training is an excellent way to stay motivated. I love rock
climbing and dirt biking, where I have to be stay focused. They sure beat
riding a stationary bike in my basement gym.

One time, a friend dropped by and suggested we take our road
bikes for a spin. I figured he meant maybe a boring twenty-miler, so I was
going to turn him down. But when he told me he had to ride more than
a hundred miles as the result of a bet, I said I was definitely in. Turned

with this friend. Tao is not just intelligent, but he sets the bar so high that people have to either concede or tear him down. He won't settle for anything less than excellence, and he knows you walk a lonely road that way.

He has created his own little industry. There's maybe only one other guy who makes real money in the sport. I don't know how many thousands of people there are trying to make money out of kayaking, but Tao is actually making a living from it. He works his butt off; that's another thing I admire about him. And he doesn't shirk. If he says he'll show up, he'll show up. There aren't many people you can count on that way.

out we took a one hundred fifty-mile bike ride over Mount Hood, even though it was only the second time I'd ever been on a road bike. (This was before I started biking as part of my training program.) It took ten hours, and I my legs were so badly sunburned that I had to tape paper bags around them for a portion of the trip. That ride was a testament to how much pain a person could take. Why did I do it? First, I just love to find new ways to test myself. Second, why not?

Beyond staying motivated, another essential is staying positive. If I believe I'll be successful, then that makes it a lot easier to succeed. I try to apply positive thinking to everything I do in life, and I believe it has helped me immensely. The night before a competition, I visualize each of my competitors and mentally list all the reasons I'm faster than they are (whether that's true or not). The goal is to put myself in a positive frame of mind just before I sleep so that when I climb into my kayak the next morning, I "know" I'm the fastest.

Malcolm Gladwell's book *Blink* quotes studies on the topic of positive thinking and outlines how it works. Likewise, a psychologist named John Bargh found that students who were asked to make sentences out of words such as *old, lonely, gray,* and *wrinkle* actually started acting old after doing the exercise.

Beyond maintaining my motivation and positive outlook, I find visualization a crucial tool, one typically underutilized in sports. Just before I race or run a waterfall, I create a clear mental picture of what I'm about to tackle and, over and over again, run a "film" through my mind of me attaining my goal safely.

I remember reading about an Olympic diver who injured herself leading up to the Olympics, thus robbing herself of the opportunity to physically train. Instead, she concentrated on visualization each day, and she ended up performing very well. The mind has so much power.

Visualization is particularly important on a waterfall I'm going to tackle only once. It's not as if there are "simulation falls-jumping" exercises; visualization is the next-best thing. It also helps me focus my energy. Because I typically close my eyes while visualizing at the top of a falls, I've learned to hold on to something at that point. Once I opened my eyes just in time to see that I got swept into the current and was near the lip of the falls. I certainly don't want my kayak to zip over while my eyes are closed!

Cameras sometimes zoom in on my face the very moment I'm doing my visualization. That's led some people to ask me if I'm praying. No, I always respond with a laugh. I'm visualizing! If I were relying purely on prayer to get me through, I'd be in trouble. Which reminds me of a joke: A preacher and a rabbi went to a boxing match together. When they saw the boxer close his eyes and lower his head for a moment before the match, the rabbi asked the preacher, "Is he praying?" The preacher responded, "Yeah, he's praying, but if he doesn't know how to box, it won't do him a damn bit of good!"

So, how do I train, specifically? I'm five foot six, and my ideal weight is 150 to 155. I first started weight training in ninth grade for wrestling. I didn't pursue serious weight training till I was in college, and at that point, I had no idea how to use it to become a better kayaker. Being a naturally inflexible kind of guy, I ended up putting on so much muscle that it was hard for me to rotate my arms and torso. In other words, I canceled out whatever flexibility I had, plus I tended to paddle before my muscles recovered from the weight lifting. Eventually, I figured it all out.

Mostly, from the moment I discovered kayaking, I've put in lots of hours in my boat. That's ultimately the best kind of training. In the early days, I'd paddle maybe four hours a day on two or three rivers. After a while, I tried paddling faster and faster to help me at upcoming races, and at some point, I allowed the word *training* into my vocabulary. Only more recently have I added lots of out-of-boat training, plus flat-water sprints in a long boat while wearing a heart monitor. After each set, I watch to see how quickly my heartbeat drops.

I always train with a heart monitor these days. It enables me to create benchmarks so I can determine whether I'm getting stronger. Without benchmarks, it's all too easy to train for months without becoming a better athlete.

Because extreme races are typically less than five minutes, I do flat-water workouts in my kayak, during which I paddle at maximum speed for three sets of five minutes on, two minutes off. Then I do ten repetitions of twenty seconds hard, ten seconds easy. Then I take one minute off and follow up with two more of the twenty-seconds–ten-seconds sets. The whole routine, including a short warm-up paddle, takes about fifty minutes.

With a gym in my basement, I'm fully set up to roll out of bed between six and eight in the morning, walk downstairs, and be done with my gym workout in about forty-five minutes. (I go to bed between eleven and midnight.) I'm a big believer in using my own body weight rather than manufactured weights; I don't want to grow too bulky or lose what little flexibility I have. When my training is in full swing, I do 300 pull-ups over the course of about thirty minutes. (My record is fifty-four in a row.) My first 100 I do with no break longer than fifteen seconds. Then I take a five-minute break and do my next 100. For my last set, I add forty-five pounds to my back. Then I work my abdominals and obliques in various ways, because they're so important for kayaking, and I throw in a number of chest, biceps, and triceps exercises.

In summer, I bike a lot, always trying to trim the twenty minutes or so it takes to race up the hill near my house. In winter, I sometimes hook my bike up to a trainer (a machine that essentially turns any bike into a stationary bike) to perform eight sets of two minutes hard, a minute easy.

Wearing my heart monitor, I try to push the heart rate up to more than 190, then bring it down to 150, then push it back up.

Of course, it's perfect having a couple of Class V rivers only ten minutes from my house. With or without paddling buddies, I typically spend forty minutes racing down five miles of hard whitewater about four days a week. I always wear my heart monitor so that I can use it to compete against myself. I also use it to make sure I'm pushing myself hard enough. As an example, on some days I may decide I want to keep my heart rate at more than 180 for the forty-minute paddle. If I see my heart rate is dropping below that, I just push myself harder. There is nothing I hate more than not living up to the training standards I set for myself. I strive to push my heart rate higher and higher so that when I race, I'm used to performing with my heart peaking at more than 190. That's all the cardiovascular exercise I figure I need. I'm a believer in concentrating mostly on short and intense rather than long workouts. But part of that is because long, easier workouts just really bore me, and I lose focus. In winter, when I can't find a paddling partner because it's only fifteen degrees out, I often tear down the river alone with ice forming on my helmet and life jacket. It can be miserable, I admit.

A mere seven-minute drive from my house is a set of 420 stairs leading up from the town of Hood River to high ground above. During the winter, when I'm training hard for spring, I take those stairs on three times a week as a fifteen-minute workout. I sprint up the stairs three times, and by the third time my legs are so tired I have to hold the hand-rail on the way back down. If I don't, I may land on my face. It's the most brutal thing I've found for my legs; they're shaking so badly by the end that I can hardly walk.

Jock Bradley

Tao can consume more food than anyone his size
I've seen—more than people twice his size.
One day he came over for Thanksgiving dinner
and filled his plate high. Then he went back for
seconds. I wouldn't have been able to get through
the first helping. You should have seen the mound
on his second plate. Halfway through that
second helping, I found out that this was his third
Thanksgiving dinner that day. I felt very honored
as a cook that he would want to come and do
more than nibble—he consumed—his last meal
of the day. That's my favorite food story.

But even during the peak of my training season, I'm done by 1 p.m.,
after a maximum of four hours of working out.

In my opinion, people often get too over-the-top trying to scientifi-
cally break down what their training regimen should involve. I just do
what feels right. I get more sleep during my hardest training times and
never take daytime naps. When you push your body as hard as I do, you
sleep well. We all have different times of the day we perform best, and part
of training is figuring that out and capitalizing on it. I know I'm most effi-
cient and energetic first thing in the morning. I've all but given up training

with other people, because I tend to push my body harder than most of my friends want to. I'd love to have a training partner, but the reality is, I've never found anyone who lives nearby who is willing to stick with me. Even when I run, I run to near muscle collapse. It's painful. Not many people want to put their bodies through that.

As a whitewater kayaker, I find that my training is heavily affected by the seasons. From December through April, I'm either training or out of the country in front of cameras. I generally appear in one video per year. Now that the Twitch series is finished, Eric Link and I have teamed up to make kayaking videos under the name PULSE with Eric as editor of videos targeted to the paddling market and distributed throughout the world.

I typically do two to three trips per winter, never for more than fourteen days at a time. It doesn't matter where I am in the world; by the end of two weeks, I'm ready to come home.

Leading up to my spring competition season, I usually have three months at home. That's where the bulk of my training has to happen, and I make that training a consistent pattern. When I don't have races coming up, I still train—just not as hard.

April through mid-June, I'm competing, currently in about six races per spring. Between the races, and from mid-June through the summer (when I get to scale back my training), I'm involved with television shows for, say, *Stunt Junkies* (the Discovery Channel), *Jeep World of Adventure Sports* (NBC), *Dateline, Ripley's Believe It or Not!,* Fox Television, and so on. I try to make myself available to whatever media are calling because I understand that it's important to my sponsors.

For the most part, my training regime is one I've found through trial and error. But once I met trainer Scott Zagarino, who has worked with numerous Olympic athletes from his base in Hood River, I began bouncing my goals and training off him. He initially tested me by introducing a workout through which he'd put numerous athletes. My first time through it, I outdid the first-time performance of everyone else he'd tested.

One ongoing challenge is maintaining workouts while traveling, which is scheduled around when water levels are right. When I'm in exotic terrain, my usual routine gets thrown out the window. All I can do are push-ups, sit-ups, and maybe a run. I've been known to do pull-ups on the high bars on buses that move airline passengers between hangars. That has as much to do with burning off energy as sneaking in some exercise between sessions of too much sitting. I've also been known to do pull-ups on tree limbs while at a remote photography site. Once, a branch broke and I ended up on my ass with a bit of a bruised cheek. Mostly, I overtrain a little before a trip so my muscles can rebuild during my travel time.

Some athletes have rituals before a competition, quasi-superstitious things they do to ensure success. I have one friend who is careful never to cuss before a race. I've heard of athletes who always brush their teeth or wear a certain shirt before a competition. I just try to ensure that my routine before a race varies as little as possible. That means going to bed a little early and getting up early enough that I won't feel rushed. And I always eat Grape-Nuts the morning of a race, simply because I know how my body reacts to them. I also drink a Red Bull right before I race. Because my pre-race routines, rituals, and diet so far have made me pretty successful, I dare not change anything. Other than that, I'm entirely unregimented and anything but serious. In fact, when I actually show up at an event, I tend to be the most laid-back goofball there, entirely capable of having a lot of fun.

There are always some uptight, less-than-friendly competitors. One time, someone yelled at me right before my race, "You're going to lose! I'm going to win!" I didn't pay any attention to him—just thought to myself, "What an idiot. Let the results speak for themselves." As it turned out, neither of us won.

It's only people who have something to prove who make fools of themselves like that. People comfortable with what they've accomplished are more easygoing. Once, following a race's final practice run, I asked Steve Fisher, a very good South African competitor, how his run had gone. He grinned slyly and said, "Perfectly."

"Well," I responded, "glad you got that one out of the way."

There's always a lot of trash talking before a race, but such exchanges are typically good-natured and lighthearted. Half of being a good racer is being able to deal with racing mentally.

Once someone handed me a cookie when I was training for a race. I said thanks and was about to take a bite when it occurred to me to ask, "Anything in this I should know about?"

"Yeah, marijuana," the guy replied.

I quickly handed it back, since I was due to be drug tested. I have no idea whether he knew I was scheduled for drug testing or not, but at least he was honest when I asked, and I guess I learned a lesson.

It's always important to know when you've learned a lesson. That, too, is part of training and going forward in your career. Once, back in 2000, I was competing at an extreme race during the Gorge Games in Hood River, and a number of media outlets were doing big features on me, including NBC and the *Oregonian* newspaper. I needed to place in the top sixteen in order to qualify for the harder extreme race taking place the next day. I found myself in a heat with three other kayakers, none of whom were very fast.

I'll destroy them all, I thought to myself with satisfaction. *All I have to do is get in front of them, then turn my boat at an angle so they all crash into the rocks on the side of the river. Then I'll sprint across the finish line and look cool.*

But when I turned sideways, one of the paddlers clipped my stern, and that spun me out. To my horror, all three of the other paddlers passed me as I was straightening my boat. There was so little distance between there and the finish line, I knew I probably couldn't recover, but that didn't stop me from trying. I managed to pass one of them, but as I came up on the other two, aiming to paddle between them for the finish line, they closed in, sandwiching me so that I couldn't even get my paddle into the water. They crossed the finish line ahead of me, and I failed to make the cut.

The race should have been easy for me. Had I kept my kayak straight, I'd have been fine. It was just plain stupid to pull that nasty trick. I deserved to lose for being overconfident. But it was still one of the most difficult losses I've ever had. It hurt so badly I could almost feel it in my gut for several days.

There's nothing like being humbled to feel a lesson driven home. It's okay to make a mistake once, I reminded myself, but if I ever try that again, I'm an idiot. And confidence is all very well, but overconfidence is deadly.

FREESTYLE

"Money doesn't lure [extreme athletes] *to the edge. . . .
The prize they want is the full-bodied thrill of
accomplishment."*

—Maryann Karinch,
*Lessons from the Edge: Extreme Athletes Show You
How to Take on High Risk and Succeed*

n 1999, at the age of twenty, I impulsively decided to tackle more than extreme kayaking. The idea came to me shortly after I set the world record in Banff National Park, Canada. For years, people in the kayak industry had been predicting my imminent demise. The only trouble was, I kept running harder and harder stuff without getting injured, let alone killed. I kept chalking up new first descents and appearing in ever more videos and television specials. The Banff achievement should have silenced my critics, but instead, I heard a new comment leveled: "He can obviously survive waterfalls, but that doesn't mean he can compete in another discipline of the sport. He doesn't have the kind of paddling skills that would win him freestyle competitions." In my experience, success always seems to breed contempt. Too often I see critics try to bring people down to their level as opposed to using others' success to raise the bar for everyone.

Well, you know me by now. A challenge is my best motivator. I rallied to this statement like a bull to a flapping red cloth. I started training for freestyle races. From a marketing point of view, this wasn't the wisest place to funnel my energies. If the world at large has barely ever seen a kayak going over a waterfall, it's far less clued-in to freestyle competition. So regardless of how many freestyle-event podiums I envisioned in my future at that point, the media were a lot more interested in my extreme exploits. Luckily, my sponsors were okay with me focusing on freestyle, although they'd have been just as happy if I hadn't.

There are probably no more than one hundred fifty competitive freestyle kayakers in all the United States, and freestyle is not yet in the X Games or Olympics. (Whitewater slalom kayaking, a very low-profile event in the Olympics, is performed in an entirely different type of kayak and is not even on freestyle or extreme kayakers' radar.)

But let me explain what freestyle kayaking is. In freestyle events, kayakers compete on a river wave the same way surfers will on an ocean wave. They perform interesting tricks that require a truly intimate feel for how to read and manipulate water hydraulics. For example, picture a controlled front loop in the air achieved by sticking the bow of one's kayak into a river feature that launches boat and paddler into the air like a rocket. If you land upright back on the water, great. If not, you do a lightning-fast roll. Kayakers who partake in freestyle are also known as "play boaters."

In my early days of kayaking, I never play-boated. I was all about running the hardest rapids and falls I could. But once I'd decided to round out my kayaking with freestyle accomplishments, I play-boated a lot for a year. Soon, I was winning events, but I failed to make the U.S. team in 1999, a requirement for paddling at the World Championships. For another long year, I trained with that single goal in mind.

Meanwhile, every week I would show up at a different race site. My sponsors weren't footing the bills for my freestyle activities, so that meant living out of my truck and commuting between the freestyle race sites and wherever I was being photographed for my extreme activities.

I didn't mind this vagrant lifestyle, of course. It was how I'd gotten by in all my early years of kayaking, right through the Central America trip. In fact, given how I grew up, I was probably way more comfortable with it than many other freestyle racers. This was still early in my kayaking career, before I was making any real money to speak of. But because I'd acquired some extreme-paddling sponsorships and a media profile by then, there was a perception that I was all "bling-bling"—that if there wasn't a nice hotel room in it, I wouldn't show up. This amused me. Obviously, a lot of people didn't know what I was all about.

Osho

When we were kids, Tao would always want to walk in the front. That's just the way he is. Even today, any group he hangs out with, he likes to be very engaged and one of the leaders, preferably the leader. Some of his critics have brought this up. He doesn't always let others rise to the occasion. Some people are threatened by that. If they don't get to know him, they see this guy who kind of runs roughshod over people and has to be the guy calling the shots.

When I finally made the U.S. freestyle team, the next step was to compete in the Pre-World Championships, which were in Spain. So after a long flight to Europe and a few hours on trains, it was time to stand by the roadside and stick out my thumb. Hours later, as the driver crested the hill into Sort, Spain, my heart sank. There was the town, but I didn't see any kayakers. Had I come to the wrong place? It turned out I was a little early. Eventually, about two hundred competitors showed up for the three-day event.

Each paddler was allowed two one-minute rides in the "hole" (the swirling whitewater hydraulic) to strut his stuff. There was no room for error. Every heat was vitally important, because one mistake would throw you out of the competition. Every time I nosed my boat into that cauldron, whatever trick I could do reflected a hard year's training. The winner would be whoever had trained hardest leading up to the event.

The first day cut the field down to fifty. Over the next two days, the competition whittled front-runners to twenty, then ten, then five, and finally to the final two. I didn't make the final cut; I came in seventh. That had people patting me on the back saying, "Great job!" but I wasn't happy. I'm never happy with anything less than first place. If you want to win, you have to go in with the winning attitude. I returned home and started training all over. It was two years before I made the U.S. team again. That same year, I won the Asian Cup and the Japanese Open. By then, needless to say, I was more than ready to fly to Graz, Austria, and compete in the 2002 Pre-World Championships.

After two days of training on Graz's river feature, I felt as ready as I was going to be. The hole in which we were competing was really difficult. It was a big, trashy hydraulic so abusive that some of the competitors got thrashed to the point that they had to eject from their kayaks and swim out of it. I made it to the last cut; there were now just five competitors left. I had to go first because I had only just squeezed into fifth place. My ride was good but far from perfect. At this point in the competition, the lowest-scoring rider is thrown out of the event, and the final four, then three, then two, advance.

Next up was Eric Jackson, two-time world champion and former Olympian for slalom kayaking. His ride was worse than mine, which meant he was out of the competition and I advanced. Second out was an Italian, followed by a Japanese competitor. Now I was going head-to-head against Jay Kincaid to see who would become the Pre-Worlds champion. Jay trains harder than anyone I know for freestyle kayaking, and even though he hadn't yet won any Worlds or Pre-Worlds championships, I considered him the best play boater in the world. (Jay would later win a world championship.) But at that point in his career, Jay always had difficulty with the pressure at big events. Later, once he got used to competing at the top events, he usually dominated.

I knew that Jay had never advanced this far at the Pre-World Championships, so I thought the pressure might trouble him. I also knew this was probably going to be the last year I could beat him, because after this event, he'd grow more comfortable with this level of competition. I'm someone who usually rises to the occasion when there is lots of pressure, and I was really counting on it that day. As I paddled into the hole on my last round, I knew I had to be near perfect over the next sixty seconds to win. It's amazing how many athletes' life achievements are defined in seconds of performance, or even fractions of seconds.

Shortly after my performance, I stood high on the top podium with the gold medal dangling from my neck, listening to the national anthem. I can't even begin to describe how good it felt to be number one. It had been my entire focus for several years. It was what I'd wanted more than anything. As I stood on the podium, I thought about all that had gone into making this moment possible. But even as the cameras flashed, I thought, *Okay, I'm finished with freestyle. I've done what I set out to do. My heart is really in extreme kayaking, and I am ready to focus on that again.*

There'd been so many winter days I'd trained in the snow, freezing my ass off, not because I'd wanted to be out testing myself but because I'd wanted to win this big event. I'd been willing to pay whatever price it took. But now that I had won, I no longer had a goal that would motivate me for further freestyle training. Besides, while in the freestyle circuit, I was on the road competing every weekend for months; from March through July, I had almost every day booked. As much as I like being busy, this was too much for me. It was time to back away from potential burnout.

The win gave me credibility in the freestyle crowd. It didn't affect my sponsorships for better or worse. My extreme kayaking generates so much more buzz and hype, it's just as well I enjoy it more. Certainly, since achieving my freestyle goals, I've never looked back.

Although my stint in freestyle was influenced by what critics were saying about me, I've learned to let most criticism roll off me. My sense is that many of my competitors want to bring me down, want to see me fail. They don't know that their attitude helps more than hurts me, because it makes me train harder and longer. But sometimes the malevolence gets unethical. For instance, I've seen Web sites where someone has posted correspondence pretending to be me. One such imposter claimed he (supposedly, I) was heading to Colorado to beat everyone and to run whitewater without scouting. Anything to make me look like a jerk. It goes with the territory; you just have to learn not to care too much about public perception on some occasions.

Once, a producer was interviewing a guy who'd participated in a Twitch video with me and asked him to talk about me. The paddler responded that he'd had all kinds of negative perceptions about me that had been dashed when he'd actually met me—that I was actually an okay guy. Well, a posse of paddlers promptly bashed this poor fellow on camera, saying he'd turned into a Tao crony. Yet none of these paddlers actually knew me themselves! So here you had people who didn't know me dissing someone who did know me for refusing to bash me. It's just one example of how ridiculous some of the circles in the paddling world are.

Racing at the Teva Mountain Games

Another example arose at a Teva Mountain Games competition, where a racer by the name of Tommy Hillicky entered in a boat that was one foot over the legal limit; it was more than thirteen feet long. Somehow, the race organizers who normally measure and approve boats missed processing his. When I came in second behind him, a number of people urged me to report him. When I did, he was immediately disqualified, at which point some of my competitors challenged me: "Hey, you got him kicked out of the race just so you could get first!" All I could think

190

was, *If it had been me trying to race in an illegal boat, the news would've hit the paddling magazines.*

Then there's the Shannon Carroll controversy, which got picked up in *Canoe & Kayak* magazine in 2006. Shannon is a skilled whitewater kayaker with whom I paddled during shooting for one of the Twitch videos. She was with me the day I ran Johnston Falls in Banff. She'd been eyeing it at the same time, contemplating running it. I'd been paddling with her for a month at that point, and I knew what she was and wasn't capable of. My team and I had helped save her life on three occasions prior to the day at Johnston. I never like seeing people paddle things that are over their heads, and in my opinion, she had a tendency to do so. Twice before the Banff run, when Shannon had climbed into her kayak to run stuff for which I believed she lacked the skills, I had said as diplomatically as I could, "You're not making the right decision." On both occasions, she had ended up agreeing and backing off. But when I did the same at Johnston Falls and then took the world record, she reported to the press that I had "messed with her head" for my own selfish reasons. It made me sad, this example of the media getting only 10 percent of the story and Shannon changing the context of what really happened.

Typically, paddlers understand what's going down better than the media. For instance, when I ran the eighty-foot waterfall in Mexico—an unofficial world record—members of our group measured it as most paddlers do, by lowering a throw rope to its pool. Six months prior to that trip, another group of paddlers (who did not run the falls) measured it at about eighty-five feet—and took a photo of the dangling throw rope.

Following news of my run, one publication published the other group's photo with the caption, "Seventy-five-foot throw bag not touching river." Several years later, another group measured the falls at about sixty-five feet, and a magazine reported this, implying that I had lied about the height of the falls. Yet, as most paddlers know and as I could have explained had anyone taken the trouble to check with me, a waterfall's height can change. It's affected by water level, season, and a host of other factors. When a hurricane hits, it can blow sand and debris into the pool below a falls, filling it so that the falls shrinks. Just recently, the Hood River rose ten feet during flooding. The idea that the falls was eighty feet when I ran it and sixty-five feet when the other group measured is entirely plausible, especially in areas with hurricanes. It's funny how the publication never checked who in my group (again, I wasn't the one) actually gauged the height.

This tendency to try to pull someone down rather than legitimately surpass them exists well beyond the realm of sports, of course; I see it in the business world, too. But I never know quite what to make of acquaintances who are very nice to me in person, then allow themselves to be quoted anonymously in articles bent on putting me in a negative light. One such individual was quoted in a *Men's Journal* article about me as saying he'd rather cut off his arm than paddle with me.

I figure it all goes back to my helping to place kayaking in the limelight, something some people in the sport aren't interested in or ready for. Many other sports have been through this phase—baseball, for instance. These days, any record set in baseball gets widespread coverage. Many kayakers aren't used to their sport being known at all, let alone having "outsiders" pay attention to records within it.

What is the future of kayaking? Well, thanks partly to the popularity of extreme-kayaking videos, people are running things previously considered unrunnable. The videos opened their eyes to what could be paddled. Shorter boats (offering more maneuverability) and new paddling techniques have also contributed to the surge in extreme paddling.

I've had the privilege of being able to watch many up-and-coming young paddlers begin to make their mark. I particularly respect Pat Keller, Dane Jackson, and Jason Craig. They are all amazing paddlers and are the future of our sport. In fact, at ages twelve and thirteen, Dane and Jason (both now fourteen) were already beating many of the men in freestyle events. Pat is running really difficult falls and rapids, and making it look easy.

Lilly

People don't know how hard he's worked for his achievements—all the training he does and the relationships he's built with his sponsors.

As is true with other extreme sports, there aren't a lot of girls. I chalk this up to the fact that girls tend to have a stronger "self-preservation gene" and prefer not to spend as much of their lives injured. Maybe that means they are just smarter or have a better perspective on what's important in life. There are definitely notable exceptions, however, such as Nikki Kelly from New Zealand and Tanya Faux from Australia. I consider both of them to have better skills than many male paddlers. But they're the exception, not the rule.

On the other hand, some of the young paddlers taking on extreme runs are paddling above their skill limits. When I see this, I have no problem suggesting they back down a little. One group paddling for the film company Teton Gravity Research went to Iceland to tackle some pretty hairy stuff. By the end of the trip, all but one paddler had ended up in the hospital with serious injuries. That's a pretty strong sign of poor judgment. One injury may reflect that a paddler is still fine-tuning where his limit is, but multiple or serious injuries send a whole different message. These days, I see a lot more kayakers injured than I used to.

Osho

Tao is very loyal. He's someone you can count on. That's something he doesn't get much credit for. If a friend were in a predicament on a river, Tao's the guy you'd want to be out there because he's the one who will put his life on the line to help you. That's just the way he is in general.

Some people think I'm balls-to-the-walls, that I'll run anything. Viewers of the videos I'm in see the action; they don't see the amount of time I spend checking out the run or conversing with the safety crew, making sure safety is well set up.

When I first started running difficult whitewater, there weren't standardized techniques for the best body position while going over a waterfall. Most kayakers used to lean back, but that never made sense to me. When you lean back, it's hard to be proactive, to react quickly. It seemed like a defensive rather than an offensive position; if you flipped while leaning back, your face was exposed to rocks under the surface of the falls. Worse, the "soft" parts of your body—all your important internal organs—are exposed. Then there's the landing factor. If you are unfortunate enough to land flat in the falls' pool while lying back or sitting upright, all that compression is going to act on your spine— strongly enough to break your back or crush vertebrae. If you lean forward, on the other hand, you remove pressure from your spine and transfer it to your buttocks, which can handle it more easily.

So I started experimenting with different body positions on small waterfalls. I decided that leaning forward was the better option. That way, if I needed to take a stroke halfway down to change the way I was falling, I could do so. And if I flipped over, then my forward tuck would protect my face, my organs, the front of my body. Only my back would be exposed.

In the early days of waterfall-jumping, people used to hold their paddles high over their heads as they left the lip of the falls. I don't know whether paddlers did it for show or theorized that the plunge into water would raise the paddle up there anyway, but to my mind, it's bad technique. It leaves your shoulders in their weakest position, which explains why many early falls-jumpers ended up blowing out their shoulders. I always keep my paddle very low so that my shoulders are at their strongest; this way they can resist the impact of the paddle blade hitting the water, which can tear your arms up if they're in the air.

In all the falls I've leapt and all the rapids I've done, I've never dislocated a shoulder. In fact, as the physio at the Red Bull training center observed, I've paddled for so long and so overdeveloped my shoulder muscles that I can't raise my arms above my head. When my shoulders rotate, they can't rotate all the way because they bump into muscle. Strange as it may sound, I think that has helped me avoid shoulder injuries. It forces me to keep my arms low, which most paddlers know is the best way to keep from blowing out a shoulder.

When a kayak sponsor sends me a boat, it's constructed so that my feet are up against hard plastic. That may be fine for bracing one's feet in whitewater rapids, but if I'm running a waterfall and land on a rock, there's not enough give to prevent my ankles from breaking. So I modify my boats for the big drops. I build in squishy foam with slits cut out of it to absorb the force of a hard impact. I've been doing this for years, and it has been so effective that there have been times I've crashed into rocks that have wrecked my kayak, yet I've walked away with barely a limp. These days, some manufacturers provide a piece of foam for this purpose, but it's still not as effective as what I insert into my boats.

A CHOSEN LIFE

"*Success is no longer measured in terms of team, or wins. Success is measured by how much the individual enjoys the experience.*"

—Arlo Eisenberg, X Games gold-medal-winning inline skater,
in *To the Extreme: Alternative Sports, Inside and Out*

O nce, Red Bull gathered seventy of its athletes in Las Vegas for a three-day party. The party's theme was a Formula 1 racing school, so we got to race Indy and Formula 1 cars, take BMWs on an off-road track, and even drag race. We also spent time gambling. I love playing blackjack. I don't throw much money at it, because when I'm in a casino, I figure any setting with that much glitter has to be a place where people lose more than win. So I keep it in moderation. I always give myself at most a $1,000 limit, but I usually quit long before I've lost that much.

Every night, we'd return to our casino hotel's "*Real World* suite" and gamble and drink till three in the morning. I remember there being lots of rooms in that suite, and I remember the male athletes periodically wandering downstairs and returning with girls from the casino they'd invited up to our party. It was a pretty crazy three days.

But as perks of the job go, here's one that was even better: *Men's Journal* once invited me to design any all-expenses-paid adventure I wanted, as long as I let the magazine send a writer and photographer along. I chose to dirt bike through Africa with Alfie Cox, an eight-time Paris-to-Dakar motorcycle racer.

More recently, *Stunt Junkies* suggested I come up with a "variation on what you do every day." *Perfect,* I thought. I've always wanted to launch out of a helicopter into a river just above a waterfall. Why? Because I figure that at some point, I'll find a drop with no other access. So the *Stunt Junkies* offer allowed me to test that scenario.

I found a three-tier waterfall near Duluth, Minnesota, the third tier being a sixty-foot drop. I proposed that the helicopter hover twenty feet above the drop as I launched out of it in my kayak.

"I want to land about seven feet above the lip of the falls," I said.

The producer agreed. So, five days after I'd scouted it, we flew there with a twenty-five-person crew—only to find that the river level had dropped substantially that week. The deepest portion of the river just above the falls now offered no more than two feet of water.

"I'd better launch from fifteen instead of twenty feet," I suggested, one eye on the waving trees that indicated yet another complication: heavy winds. The pilot nodded obligingly.

"Remember to launch with your paddle horizontal," the pilot reminded me soberly. "If you raise it vertically, it could catch in the rotor blades and bring the entire helicopter down."

"Right," I agreed, knowing that I also had to land the kayak flat. If I "penciled" in, the bow of the boat would hit rocks. It was also crucial to land right side up, as there'd be no time to roll before my boat went over the falls.

Osho

He's a total salesman, a better salesman than I am.
He's always been one. He'll admit it, too.

I sat in my kayak on the floor of the noisy helicopter as the pilot lifted us to the desired position. With the door open, all I had to do was count down aloud and launch myself out.

"Three, two ..." Suddenly, a gust of wind moved the entire helicopter ten feet to the right, and I found myself staring down at rocks covered by less than six inches of water.

"Abort!" I shouted. Twice I had to abort the countdown and wait for the pilot to reposition us, all the time reminding myself to keep my paddle horizontal and land flat. There was so much to concentrate on at once.

The third time, I tipped forward, paddle horizontal, and plunged fifteen feet. What I hadn't anticipated was how much of a hurricane force the rotors would exert on the water. This blew me off line, but at least I landed flat and was able to correct my line partway down the falls.

So the jump was successful; the crew was happy with the footage. And me? I'm all about trying to find something really, really difficult and

Dirt-biking in Africa for a *Men's Journal* story

then looking at it like a puzzle: how can I pull this off without getting injured? I've been dropping over falls for years, but this was truly a challenging variation, and getting to do it was a great perk. My career seems full of perks these days; I often feel really fortunate.

Then there's the topic of girls. Because I'm fit, single, and an incurable flirt, I have a reputation for getting around way more than I actually do. It's really not my thing. I prefer to find a good girl whom I can trust and stick with her. The problem is just finding one. It's true that in my line of work, I come across a lot of good-looking girls willing to give me their phone numbers. But that doesn't necessarily mean they'll like me once I ask them out, nor does it follow that I'll like them once I get to know them. Besides, I'm not interested in girls who give me their numbers just because of my career.

Anyway, whether because of my upbringing or the demands of my career, I'm very, very particular about whom I date. Though I'm the first to admit I'm a big flirt around females, for me, it's a very big jump from flirting to dating. For one thing, I'm never sure exactly what girls are after. It's pretty tricky to figure out what a girl is after in any circumstance, but given that I'm a little bit of a celebrity and have a four-thousand-square-foot house and a bunch of cool toys, I find myself particularly wary. That, and I've seen some friends get pretty worked over by girls. Or maybe it's just my excuse for being scared of commitment. I don't take every girl home that I could. I'm not into girls knowing my life. I've always kind of hoped I could find a girl who doesn't know anything about me. Someone who I would know liked me just for me, and not for my money, accomplishments, or career. As happy and carefree as I may be on the surface, I'm a pretty private person underneath. When I'm flying between paddling stints and someone asks me what I do, I often say "business" just to keep from having to recite the story of my unusual career and get the 100 questions that follow.

Once, I was at a party after a kayak race, following a crowd onto the dance floor as people laughed and downed drinks. One minute I was dancing with some girl I didn't know, and the next, she was kissing me and taking her shirt off as people whistled and clapped. That was it. A little too strange a scene for me. I wanted nothing to do with her, so I turned and walked off the dance floor. I was pretty tired anyway, so I headed toward camp, ready to crawl into my tent for some shut-eye. Hardly had I zipped myself into my sleeping bag when she opened the flap and flopped down beside me.

Good grief! What was it going to take to get rid of this chick? I rose and walked her to her tent, my hand on her elbow to steady her wavering gait. Of course, you can imagine what people were saying back at the dance.

Another time, I arrived at a party fully intending to drive home a few hours later. But I ended up drinking a little more than I had planned, and by the small hours of the morning, I knew I shouldn't drive, even though I had nowhere to stay but in my car with no sleeping bag. Three girls who learned of my plight offered me their tent. Dead tired and grateful, I accepted, sleeping from 5 to 7 a.m. with three girls in a two-person tent. Yes, we slept—that's it—not that anyone believed me.

While racing in Russia once, I flirtatiously put my arm around a girl at a party just as a magazine photographer clicked his shutter. When the photo appeared, it sure didn't go over very well with my girlfriend at the time.

I've learned it comes with the territory, these winks and old-boy slaps on the back where none are due. As if an athlete is by definition an alpha male in the sexual as well as the sports sphere. Seems that if I walk

Lilly

Tao probably likes girly girls because none of us were that way growing up. We didn't have power or running water. I curled my hair with a butane curling iron. I wasn't a tomboy, but I didn't primp, either—nor did Mom. Tao may say he likes a girly girl, but she'd have to be a girl who can keep up with him, too—one who isn't afraid to try new things or be on her own.

down the street with a girl, people assume I'm sleeping with her. If they see me walking with a different female two days later, tongues start wagging again. Now, I'm not saying I'm a saint. In fact, far from it. I just don't like girls who I think are interested in me just because of my career. There have been moments in my life I've gone a little wild, but generally speaking, that's not me. I don't open up easily to anyone, girls least of all. I've had only three real relationships with girls in my twenty-eight years of life, although plenty of flings in between.

The first, as I mentioned, was with Robin at age fifteen; I eventually had to promise not to see her in order for her evangelical-Christian control-freak dad to let her out of the house.

My second long-term girlfriend was Jen, older sister of my longtime paddling buddy Josh Bechtel. All it took was seeing her photo during a

Filming a show for Discovery Channel where I was launching out of a helicopter into a three-tiered waterfall

visit to Josh's house. I said, "Wow, she's hot. I'd like to meet her." I didn't even think to ask if she was single. Josh just grinned and handed me her number. I was twenty at the time, and she was twenty-two. I figure Josh was fine with me going after his sister because I'm a pretty good guy. I don't cheat on girls. I'm loyal to the ones I date, and I take good care of them—try to, anyway. I have commitment issues, yes, but hey, I was only twenty then. Not a problem, especially with Josh.

So I phoned Jen and left a message, then departed to shoot in Canada the next day. When I returned, I was just sorting through my junk when the phone rang. She sounded pretty enthusiastic about getting together. I arranged to pick her up and take her to the local carnival. When I showed up at her house, I discovered she was even hotter than in the photo. She's a petite blonde with blue eyes and a fantastic body. She was wearing a skirt; a cute, tight-fitting top; lots of makeup and jewelry; and a big, easy smile. I knew instantly she had a fun personality, and I was right. It never felt like a blind date, not for a minute. We just connected and started climbing aboard all the carnival rides, laughing and cheering and talking with ease. She was boisterous, happy, and positive, and she loved to have a good time.

We were only a few days into the relationship when, as I was leaving her place, she called out sleepily, "I love you." I froze in my tracks. She gazed up, caught the look on my face, and said, "Sorry, sorry! I didn't mean to say that!"

The relationship nearly died right then and there, but I ended up deciding to overlook her outburst. We dated for more than two years. Initially, I was living in Ashland, Oregon, and she was in Seattle. We spent lots of time on the phone. When things didn't work out for her in Seattle, I said, "Why don't you move down?" I didn't mean move in with me—hell, no. She had a friend she could move in with.

I remember lots of good times. She was one of the most fun girls I've ever hung out with. But gradually, I saw a selfish and uptight side to her that made me conclude she wasn't the one for me. Besides, I was far from ready to settle down. We were on our way to a race in Colorado when we stopped in Moab, Utah, to rent a topless 4x4. As we headed out into the backcountry, we got lost, it started to rain, and I realized we were nearly out of gas. A part of me was thinking, "All right! An adventure! I wonder how this will play out?"

But to Jen, it was a disaster worth going nearly hysterical. She got crazier and crazier, not contributing to a solution at all. I couldn't help reflecting: *If things ever get tough in life, this is how she's going to deal with it—freaking out instead of being helpful.* It was the beginning of the end. To me, it's the little things people do that define their personalities. The little things are harder for someone to hide. It didn't help that she wanted to marry me and have kids. And it didn't help when she said she'd never marry without a prenuptial agreement. *If we got married and then divorced,* I thought, *she's the kind who'll take me to the cleaners.* The breakup was all the stickier for the fact that she was living with Josh Bechtel's girlfriend at the time, but he never let it come between us. He's a really good guy that way.

Three weeks after Jen and I broke up, she started dating someone else. That hurt. All I could think was, *How could a girl want to marry you and have your kids one month and be with another guy the next month?*

It was almost three years before I got into a steady relationship again.

So, what kind of girls do I like? I like someone who's genuine and loyal, a girl with a good heart, not someone who is always trying to position things so they're best for her. I like girly girls, the kind who wear makeup, but not too much, and like to get their toenails painted, yet are also active and love going to cool places in the world. They like to go out and have a good time, and of course, it's a no-brainer that they're physically fit and cute.

I'd never date a girl who kayaks. That's because I like my private life, and if I date someone in the industry, it won't be so private anymore. Ideally, I like girls who prefer to do what's best for me, not just them, and I don't take advantage of that. Ideally, I'm the same way back to them, and that makes for a healthy relationship.

For years, I've watched my friend Eric Link raise his two children, and spending time with that close-knit family has definitely made me realize I want to be a dad someday. I hope to have two kids: a boy, then a girl. The boy will have to watch his little sister so that if anyone's trying to hit on her he can pound them! I'd like a little boy to take out dirt biking and skiing and rock climbing. And if he does extreme sports, I'll be doing them with him. I can't imagine a more wonderful experience. But I want

Grandma Doreen

Tao was born with confidence, and born to parents who believed in making their children independent and self-sufficient. He's also an enormously compassionate and empathetic young man. I think he gets that from both of his parents.

kids when I have more time for them; I don't want to be a distant father. I want to be part of my children's lives all the time, like a little buddy.

I want to be sufficiently financially independent that I can spend lots of time with my kids instead of going to work if I want to. And I want to share the parenting experience, but I'm traditional in that I'll probably leave most of the child-rearing to my wife the first few years. I don't think I have the patience for lots of time with babies. But I like to imagine taking my wife and child to Italy and renting a little villa there for a year. That would be cool to experience with a family.

Thanks to my paddling career, I've traveled the world many times over, and I've always found it interesting to observe how much freedom other cultures give young children. Some have seven-year-olds babysitting their younger siblings. In our culture, parents resist giving kids responsibility until the midteen years—then parents let the kids get into a car or make big decisions that the kids haven't been groomed to handle. Even fifty to a hundred years ago, our culture entrusted children with important decision-making at younger ages than now. When I have children, I will ensure they have more freedom and responsibility than most. Kids are only as responsible as you help make them be. They can't always rise to the occasion on their own.

At the same time, like my brother, Osho, I think perhaps we had a little too much freedom, so I would try to give my children more structure and discipline. In stark contrast to how we were raised, my sister, Lilly, is living the all-American life: married with a kid and totally into being a terrific mom. That's pretty different from the life I'm leading, and I'm probably a bad uncle because she lives in Seattle and I'm away from the Northwest so often. But I'm sure there will come a time I can be a bad influence on my young nephew.

If I wanted to have this career and kids at the same time, I could. When I travel, I'm not gone for all that long, and when I'm home, I'm home 24-7. But commitment with a woman freaks me out. The day I propose, I imagine I'll be more nervous than I've ever been at the lip of a drop or the start of a race.

My most serious relationship took root shortly after I moved to Hood River, Oregon, in 2004. Hood River was the first town that felt like home to me. It's where I've bought a house on a hill with a spectacular view of Mount Hood. It's where I hope to stay. Before I moved to Hood River, anywhere I lived felt like somewhere to train, somewhere to hang out between travels.

The Halloween after I arrived in Hood River, I went to a party dressed as a cheerleader. Honest! I've learned over the years that when you go to a costume party dressed like a chick, the cutest chicks at the party gather around and want to talk with you. Anyway, I'm no good at planning costumes, and dressing like a girl is easy if you have female friends willing to lend you some clothes. So I entered this house party in Portland, Oregon, with a miniskirt, a tight-fitting top and pom-poms. I'd even managed to pull on black stockings and high heels.

Right away, I noticed a girl at the far end of the room dressed as a bunny. Her costume was nothing very fancy, just bunny ears. I initially assumed she was a Playboy bunny. Later, I'd be chagrined to learn she was only trying to be a bunny. She had beautiful dark hair, olive skin, a very pretty face, and a great body. She was the prettiest girl at the party, and I gravitated toward her as if she were the only one there. I have no idea how I kicked off a conversation, but I remember how she smiled at me; I remember her soft brown eyes and perfect Italian complexion. When

Osho

Tao is a lot more relaxed than he was in his teens. In his teens, he was pretty uptight and critical of people who were doing things he didn't approve of or that didn't interest him [such as partying]. He still exercises strong discipline and restraint, but he's more open to different ideologies. But getting Tao to open up is superhard. He's been presented with the same questions a million times, so he has these punch lines. He's always been like that. It comes off very canned and rehearsed.

I started to tell her my name, she told me she already knew. I remember talking with her effortlessly all evening, as if no one else existed. I remember thinking how down-to-earth she was, and how hard that is to find. Her name was Jamie, and she was a paralegal in Portland.

It wasn't far into the evening that I asked for her phone number. I wasn't terribly nervous; I was pretty sure she was at least interested enough to give me her number. Then I asked her if she'd come to my place for dinner some night. She said yes.

I prepared a steak dinner, complete with homemade steak sauce. She seemed impressed, if only because she didn't know yet that it is one of the few meals I know how to pull off. After dinner, when I figured my credibility in the cooking department was high, I brought out a plate of raw octopus, all seasoned and garnished, and pretended it was ready to eat. She knew better right away and laughed as I'd hoped she would.

Shortly after that first date, I flew to Argentina for some video work. Jamie and I e-mailed each other every day. When I returned, I couldn't wait to see her again.

We dated for three years, burning up the road between Portland and Hood River. Soon she was visiting every weekend, even preparing meals on Sunday evenings to leave for my weekday suppers. She accompanied me on a trip to Mexico for a television show, which made it feel like a special vacation even though I was working. Another time, we went for ten days with twenty friends to Baja, where we surfed, ran, and biked together.

She was very rational and sensible, always saving money for her retirement and the future. When we'd been dating for a year, I gave her a gold necklace with a heart on it. She loved that necklace; she wore it every day. We continued dating for another two years, until the summer of 2007.

She was considerate, kind, and genuine. We always had good times together. She spoiled me. I knew she was the best girl I'd ever met, and I knew—I still know—I might never find anyone better. She was so caring; she'd do anything for me. But she was thirty-five, and I was twenty-eight. She never put pressure on me about marriage or children. She didn't need to. I simply knew it was not fair to continue the relationship if I couldn't commit to those, and I was not ready. The breakup was very, very tough. It would have been so much easier if there had been something clearly wrong between us, something worthy of a quarrel.

The end of our last weekend together, she pulled on her coat and, without meeting my eyes, turned to gaze at Mount Hood through my living room's two-story picture window. Her eyes lingered there, as if committing the view to memory. Then she turned and walked slowly out the door. That was one of the worst moments of my life. I went upstairs and sat down, numb but unable to show my emotions. Something in my bedside waste-basket caught my eye. I leaned closer. It was the heart necklace.

My inability to commit to relationships is one of my bad qualities. I just can't commit. My name is Tao-can't-commit Berman. It's not related to what I do for a living. A part of it may be my parents' separation when I was four. My only memories of them together are of their fighting. Dad has found another partner, and she seems like a wonderful woman; she's good for him. But I'm an analytical, rational person, and sometimes it seems all I see is divorce around me. I like my life the way it is now, and I see what people's lives are like when they go through a divorce. I guess it seems easier not to get married than to see people go through what I went through growing up.

The other part is that I'm very motivated and goal oriented, and being in a committed relationship has never taken priority over my career and what I want to accomplish. I believe I'll marry one of these days. I don't have an age in mind, although I don't want to be the forty-year-old bachelor. I like to think that someday I'll find a girl I like so much that I'll do anything for her. When I find that girl, I'll stay with her.

My commitment phobia is one of my shortcomings. I know it nega-tively impacts my potential happiness because I like to think long-term. Jamie was one of the few people on earth I completely trusted and could tell anything to. When we broke up, I lost not just my girlfriend, but also one of the few people who knows everything I'm doing, one of the very few with whom I could share anything.

On the other hand, the advantage of being single again is that I can do whatever I want whenever I want. I'm in the process of selling my house and building another on a nearby lot. The new one will be large enough to give my mother a retirement suite if she ever needs to come live with me. It won't have a hot tub; I think hot tubs are overrated. I sit in them only if I'm sore; they make me tired, and I hate feeling tired. Anyway, if I sell my current house before the new house is constructed, I'll wing it the way only a bachelor could, maybe parking a travel trailer on the new lot. That sounds kind of appealing right now.

As I've mentioned, one of my hobbies is plotting my finances. I especially like investing: I like analyzing portfolios, looking at risk relative to return, tax implications, fees, etc. For some reason, I find this stuff interesting and fun. It's interesting to me to look at historical rates of return so I know what something is likely to be worth fifteen to thirty years down the line. I got interested in reading books on investing when I was eighteen. I remember one book revealing that if you start saving for retirement at twenty-seven instead of thirty-five, you'll end up with twice as much money. That's because money invested in the stock market doubles roughly every eight years.

Athletes are known for being big spenders, but my focus has always been on saving for the future. I'm ever aware that I'm only one injury away from forced retirement. My biggest expense is taxes. Other than that, there are vacations, food, and motorcycles. (Even though I get some motorcycles free from sponsors, I also buy some, and then there's the gas, maintenance, and repair.) I'm definitely not a materialistic person compared with many other athletes. Chalk that up to the frugality of my parents and my desire to be financially independent if an accident were to end my career earlier than planned. Anyway, I don't like possessions or toys to control me because of debt. I've always put a priority on saving first and then buying toys after I've achieved my savings goal for

Mom

When Tao was first born, Birch took him and held him for maybe six hours. Tao was Birch's first child, and he was beside himself with happiness. The whole birth was amazing to him.

When Birch and I first split up three years later, Tao and Osho cried a lot. I'd never really heard them cry before. There was a lot of sadness, and Tao was always angry. I think Tao was very bonded to his father. He wasn't bonded to me at all. I had to work with that. I had to wrap myself around him, regain him.

The split was very painful for me. I can't imagine what it must have been like for such tiny children.

the year. I know that blowing large amounts of money isn't what really makes me happy. That said, I do enjoy my toys; the current lineup is an Audi, a BMW, a WRX, a street bike, and two dirt bikes. But the WRX was given to me by Subaru, and one of the motorcycles was given to me by KTM. My toys for cross-training are two mountain bikes, two road bikes, a workout gym, downhill skis, ten to fifteen kayaks, and climbing gear.

Then there were many years where Birch and I didn't get along. More recently, Birch and I have made a bit of peace. We've been really loving toward one another. At Osho's graduation in 2007, Birch and his partner and I were all talking and laughing and having a really good time. I looked over and saw Tao watching us intently. Only the night before, he'd said, "Don't ever talk to me about Dad," because he was afraid I'd say something negative. All of sudden he gave us this huge smile. I've never seen Tao smile like that in my life. I think he found permission to relax; he doesn't need to protect something anymore.

I've found that what makes me happiest is spending time with my good friends and not being stressed. My only weakness, perhaps, is fast cars. Nevertheless, I have a hard time justifying buying something I'll be bored with in three months. Too many Americans subscribe to the notion, "Why wait for tomorrow's dream when you can have it today?" They don't realize how debt and high interest payments can cramp their lifestyles and limit their options. What I mean by that is, if you have a lot of debt and you hate your job, you may not be able to pursue a more-meaningful career because your monthly debt payments are too high for you to go without a paycheck, even for a short time.

I also think people over rely on financial advisers for handling their retirement savings. Why spend forty hours a week earning money only to entrust it to someone you hardly know? Wall Street is the only place where a guy driving a Rolls-Royce will take advice from one who rides the subway to work. Most financial planners are glorified salespeople. They awake every morning wondering how to make more money for themselves—not necessarily for their clients. Non–actively managed index funds have outperformed about 90 percent of funds managed by professionals for the past thirty years. This is why I do all my financial planning for myself, as well as for some of my friends. It's easy to ensure you have plenty of money for retirement if you start planning while young.

I'm as risk averse in personal finances as I am risk loving on the water. Why? I figure my shelf life is maybe ten more years at most. I don't want to be like those Super Bowl athletes I've heard about who end up pumping gas. I want to be financially smart now so that when I hang up my paddle, it prompts no life crisis. I want to plan ahead, structure my finances so that I'm ready for that day. I'm a risk taker, not a gambler. Risks can be calculated and analyzed. Gambling is throwing dice.

Although I'm not naive as to the degree of risk in my activities, I haven't planned specifically for what happens if I end up in a wheelchair. I figure the minute I start planning for a disability, I will get injured. I can't have any doubts crowding my mind when I tackle challenging whitewater. That being said, however, I've tried to buy disability insurance. I've talked with Lloyd's of London several times. The first time, they turned me down.

The second time, they gave me a quote that was so outrageous I knew it wasn't worth doing. So I continue to just play it smart with my money. If I were forced out of paddling today, I wouldn't be financially ruined.

I've been so focused on paddling since the age of fourteen, especially since going professional at eighteen, that it has definitely affected my social life. Even back in high school, I'd return from school, do my home-work, and then go paddle. I had no social life with kids my age because all that mattered to me was kayaking. Especially given that I hung out with people ten years older on the occasions I did socialize, I entirely missed out on the stage where one goes partying and gets hammered. In college, I missed parties in order to train and get to bed early, I didn't drink at all, and I never had the social life most college kids have. Though it furthered my career, it made me pretty one-dimensional for a long time. These days, I've loosened up. Nowadays, I party and drink. But I still try not to get too wild with it, at least most of the time.

As I approach thirty, I figure I know myself pretty well. I know my strong and weak points, and sometimes they're one and the same. For instance, I'm supermotivated, and that's one reason I compete success-fully. The downside is, I don't always know when to quit. Not long ago, I was at an auction where the auctioneer was asking $20 for a $60 rescue rope in a throw-bag. I got so caught up in bidding against some other guy that I ended up buying it for $150. Never mind that I could have called a sponsor and gotten one for free; obviously, I still hate to lose a competi-tion! Another time, I spent $1,000 at an auction.

Even now, if I calculate that six months of hard training will help win me a season of races but prevent me from having as much fun in my social life, I'd still go with the hard training. Then again, winning is part of having a good time, so it's not a total disconnect. But my level of training definitely makes it difficult to build and maintain close friendships.

I'm also extremely analytical. Very little I do in life is based on emotion. That contributes to my lack of fear, which allows me to do what I do. It has also helped keep me safe and uninjured. It's good, too, in that it stops me from blowing money when I'm hanging out with athletes who are spending big-time. But that all-analysis and no-emotion stuff can also lead to difficult decisions such as the one to break up with Jamie.

My level of focus has another downside: it's difficult to build and maintain close friendships. I've had friends who knew me before I gained a media profile tell me that I never open up to them anymore or that they no longer understand me. They probably have a point; sometimes I don't understand me, either, or understand the way I act when I'm feeling a need to be out of the media and public eye. It makes some people conclude I'm standoffish, which they read as egotistical. When people gather and hang out after paddling, I'm more than likely rushing off to another event or turning in early for rest and relaxation. It looks as if I'm totally into my own thing; it makes me difficult to get to know.

I can't really identify with many people, and when strangers seem interested in knowing about my life, it prompts me to pull back a little to protect my privacy. When I recently did a shoot in South America, I made $25,000 for five days of work. Because that's what many kayakers make in a year, I couldn't share that information even with some of my best friends. I want to be able to hang out with them as a peer; I don't want stark differences like that to drive a wedge between us. I'm doing something that they can't relate to or that they wish they were doing. It causes discomfort. The further you move toward the top, the lonelier it gets. I feel more at ease with top guys in other sports, such as the Bostrom brothers of motorcycling fame. Because we're at a similar level and doing similar things in our own ways, we can hang out and have a good time. As for nonathletes—people doing nine-to-five jobs—it's sometimes hard to identify with them, and hard for them to identify with me. This compounds the occasional feeling of isolation, and it probably explains why I value the few close friends I have and why I don't open up easily to others.

Dad

My overriding concern was character, which comes down to ethics and integrity. I'm extremely satisfied with how both Tao and Osho have turned out. I wanted them to have the capacity to think for themselves. I never wanted them to take anything as necessarily the way it had to be—including anything I might tell them. I always said, "If you disagree, just make damn sure you have a good rationale."

Ironically, I've had friends tell me that since I've become a public figure, I've changed. I don't think I've changed at all. I think that the media attention has simply changed friends' perception of me. It reminds me of the Joe Walsh song "Life's Been Good." One friend not long ago told me he never calls me anymore because he doesn't like to bug me. Bug me? That's ridiculous. He's precisely the guy I want to hear from!

Then there are people who like to pretend they're my friends. They'll boast to friends of mine that they know "*Tah*-o." Of course, by pronouncing my name wrong (I'm "*Tay*-o"), they're giving themselves away from the start. Once, I was dining with Josh Bechtel and other friends when a guy wandered over to Josh and said, "Hey, I met Tao last week!"

"Really?" Josh replied innocently. When the others at the table started cracking up, the guy looked around, finally recognized me, and turned an interesting shade of red.

Lilly

Our childhood shaped us into how we are now. It was a great way to be raised even though it was very unusual. We really know what we want out of life and how to get it—Tao especially.

Once, when I was traveling, the house sitter ended up throwing a party at my house. When I returned, I noticed that people had been going through my private stuff. It's hard to know whom to trust sometimes. Occasionally, athletes who make it big drop out. They disappear precisely because they can't handle that intrusion. You have to develop a thick skin. I don't mind being in the public eye to a certain extent, but it can have a downside, for sure. I'm not interested in gaining the level of fame that some big-time athletes or movie stars have. I can't imagine how old it would get to be mobbed everywhere you went.

On the positive side, I do have a few close friends. They keep me in check. They don't have a problem with telling me when I'm being a punk. Among my closest friends are my brother Osho, Eric Link, Christian Knight, Josh Bechtel, and Jock Bradley. Osho and I talk all the time. He's a top-selling salesman for a $4 billion company. I love to hear his tales of big wins and goals. It's fun to watch his success; I live the high-powered salesman's life vicariously through him. He is also a very good submission fighter. In fact, he beat a guy who went on to become the Washington state champion. But we don't do a lot of sports together, and I know he worries about the risks I take. I tell him everything about what I'm doing anyway. He's one of the few people with whom I can share anything. I don't tell my mother all that I'm doing in my kayak. I don't even tell her every time I leave the country. I know Osho and Lilly and my Grandma Doreen worry. Even Christian has told me that I worry him at times. I've always been more of a risk taker than Christian. He has more prudence. He has always tried to talk me out of doing stuff, saying things such as, "I have a bad feeling about this one."

Eric Link, on the other hand, never says that. He knows what I'm capable of doing and believes that if I think I can do it, then I can do it. On rare occasions, he'll say, "I'm not sure about this one." That's when I know I'm really pushing the envelope, but it doesn't stop me. I actually like it because it makes me even more motivated to do whatever I'm planning.

As I write this, Eric is busy putting the final touches on a DVD featuring paddling friends and me doing some hard paddling all around the world. I have the paddling skills and contacts; he has the videography skills and experience, distribution infrastructure, and music.

In the ten years we've worked together, Eric has also become a valuable resource for finding first descents. He scours topographical maps looking for rivers with enough gradient to possibly offer extreme whitewater. When he finds one, he'll go videotape it and show me the footage so we can discuss whether it's navigable. If I'm interested, off we go, me paddling, Eric shooting. Now that he's established a strong niche for himself, he sometimes gets random e-mails or photos from people around the world suggesting that he shoot me running this or that exciting drop or waterfall. Sometimes this communication comes from whitewater rafting outfitters looking for publicity. If he ends up videotaping me on these drops, we usually acknowledge our helpful sources in the DVD; sometimes Eric pays them. And if I come up with something or a major television network contacts me, you can bet that it's Jock and Eric I phone first.

Jock is someone else I hang with a lot. When Jock stopped paddling, years after we met, it didn't affect our friendship. Today, 90 percent of Jock's photography involves ocean kayaking and fishing. When he shoots whitewater, I'm usually the paddler. I'm fortunate to have worked with Jock, arguably the best photographer in the industry. His photos of me have ended up on many magazine covers and make up a large portion of his stunning new coffee-table book, *Torrent.* Better yet, we now live in the same area (near Hood River), which means I can continue to enjoy his company and his amazing cooking.

Beyond maintaining my still-busy schedule and socializing more than earlier in my career, I am looking at using my fitness and love of competition to benefit more charitable causes.

I'm getting ready to compete at a running race at about 9,000 feet for Athletes for a Cure. I got the photo taken before starting because afterward I was in no condition to be photographed.

In 2007, I participated in the Teva Mountain Games charity race in Vail, Colorado, to raise money and awareness for prostate cancer. Prostate cancer affects one in six men. That was great, being able to use my name to celebrate a worthy cause. It's important to me if I can make a small difference in helping researchers get closer to a cure. In the past, I've spoken at schools about making positive choices, but I'd never done anything quite like the Teva event.

The first race demanded that I sprint downriver in a kayak for twenty-five minutes. A few hours later, I pumped a mountain bike for two hours and thirty-five minutes, gaining between five thousand and ten thousand feet in elevation. The next morning, a ten-kilometer running race involved several thousand feet of climbing, and within a few hours, I was competing in a forty-five-minute road-bike race. All of these competitions started at about eight thousand feet, a real challenge given that I do all my training at sea level. Plus, because my usual training concentrates on the upper body, I was carrying more weight than most of my competitors, who typically had huge legs and skinny upper bodies. The race was definitely one of the most difficult I've done.

Osho

Make sure you put in the book that we're both
eligible bachelors and I have bigger biceps.
And I'm better looking despite what you say.

To help me do my best in that race, I agreed to a short-term contract with GNC, the nutrition company, because it was a good fit. The vitamins and protein they make helped me achieve my training goals for that race.

So, I've reached a point in my career where I can focus on what I'm going to do next. When I'm ready to move on, I'll start looking at opportunities that present themselves: hosting a television show, giving motivational speeches, selling real estate, doing sales or financial planning, maybe even pursuing politics. I have lots of interests outside of kayaking; I'm just not ready to focus on them yet. In fact, the closer I get to possible retirement, the more I appreciate that I'm still able to do what I do. I love the sport and plan to continue being a professional kayaker for at least the next five to ten years. Although I know that one day I won't be on top of the sport, for now I'm in the best shape I've ever been in; I recently did 500 pull-ups in one workout. I love the sport. I love to win. And I won all the races I entered this past year. That gives me a lot of satisfaction. Anyway, I could never sit around doing nothing. If I didn't have a reason or purpose for waking up each morning, I'd go crazy. I believe in finding something I'm passionate about and pursuing it with everything I've got. That certainly worked for me with kayaking.

APPENDIX

A Brief History of Kayaking

AD 1000: By this time, and possibly much earlier, natives of the arctic regions of Asia, North America, and Greenland have built the first kayaks from driftwood and animal skins. The word *kayak* means "hunter's boat."

Sixteenth century: Europeans discover the Inuit (then called Eskimo) kayak, with its partly enclosed deck and compartments for storing seals that had been harpooned.

Seventeenth century: French explorers adopt Native Americans' birch-bark canoe.

1845: Scottish lawyer John MacGregor designs the *Rob Roy,* a canoe with a deck, mast, sail, and paddles. He travels around Europe and the Middle East with it and writes about his travels in several books, starting in 1849. MacGregor is largely credited with establishing canoeing as a recreational sport.

1866: MacGregor founds what becomes the Royal Canoe Club, which launches competitive canoeing through regattas, beginning in 1867.

1871: New York Canoe Club is founded.

1880: American Canoe Association is founded.

1900: Canadian Canoe Association is founded.

1905: A German builds the first collapsible kayak based on an Inuit design, and a tailor named Hans Klepper buys the patent to establish a wood-and-canvas "foldboat" business.

1924: Canoeists from across Europe establish an international canoe club that becomes the International Canoe Federation in 1946. Also in 1924, the Paris Olympics features canoeing as a demonstration sport.

1928: Captain Fran Romer paddles and sails a kayak almost four thousand miles from Lisbon, Portugal, to St. Thomas in the Virgin Islands. He survives two hurricanes along the way.

1931: Viennese kayaker Adolf Anderle performs a first descent of the Salzachofen Gorge on the Salzach River in Austria, helping inspire the International Scale of River Difficulty (Classes I–VI) still used today.

1936: Flat-water racing becomes a full-fledged Olympic sport.

1938: Geneviève de Colmont becomes the first woman to kayak the rapids of the Colorado and Green rivers.

1948: The Olympics introduces its first women's paddling event (500-meter singles kayak).

1950s: First fiberglass kayaks are manufactured.

1968: The U.S. Canoe Association is founded to govern and sanction marathon canoe and kayak racing.

1971: Walt Blackadar does a first solo descent of Turnback Canyon on the Alsek River in northwestern British Columbia, Canada, featured in *Sports Illustrated* the following year.

1972: Whitewater racing appears in the Olympics for that year only.

1975: Three kayakers run the Spout of the Great Falls on the Potomac River: Tom McEwan, Wick Walker, and Dan Schnurenburger.

1976: Dr. Mike Jones leads a whitewater kayaking expedition tackling the Dudh Kosi, a river running off Mount Everest, for a Leo Dickinson film.

1977: Jim Snyder, Mike Fentress, and Phil Coleman run the Quarry Run tributary of the Cheat River in West Virginia, Coleman nearly paying for this first descent with his life. "First descents" in whitewater kayaking are becoming ever more common.

1981: ABC Sports films Rob Lesser and four other expert kayakers (Don Banducci, Lars Holbek, Rick Fernall, and John Wasson).

1988: Tom Visnius and John Kennedy achieve a first run of the narrows of the Green River near Asheville, North Carolina. Dave "Psycho" Simpson shocks many by being the first to canoe it a year later.

1991: The first world rodeo competition (later called freestyle) takes place in Wales, United Kingdom.

1992: Whitewater racing is restored to the Olympics.

1993: The first Ocoee River, Tennessee, World Championships mark the birth of whitewater freestyle as practiced today.

1997: The whitewater community is shocked when four prominent experts, all paddling Class V on different rivers, die within three months of one another: Rich Weiss, Dugald Bremner, Henry Filip, and Chuck Kern.

1999: Tao Berman successfully clears Alberta's 98.4-foot Upper Johnston Falls, the world record for a vertical falls.

2002: A team led by Scott Lindgren tackles a first descent of the Tsangpo in Tibet, a trip featured in Peter Heller's book *Hell and High Water: Surviving Tibet's Tsangpo River.*

2002: Tim Gross paddles himself over Oregon's 101-foot Abiqua Falls—but is washed from his kayak.

2003: Ed Lucero attempts 105.6-foot-high Alexandra Falls in the Northwest Territories—but swims from his boat at the bottom.

2003: The Whitewater Hall of Fame is established.

2004: Australian kayaker Michael O'Shea runs a source-to-sea descent of the gorges of the Mekong River, Tibet to Vietnam.

2007: Tyler Bradt runs Alexandra Falls, measured at that time at 107 feet, on September 7.

ABOUT THE AUTHORS

Tao Berman holds three world records, including one of the two world-record waterfall-descent records of 98.4 feet. He has also completed more than fifty first descents of rivers and was a Pre-Worlds champion for freestyle kayaking competition.

He has starred in many extreme-sports videos and on TV programs, including *Dateline NBC*, CNN's World Sports "Play of the Day," and two episodes of Discovery Channel's *Stunt Junkies*. He's also been featured in *Sports Illustrated*, *Men's Journal*, *Rolling Stone*, and *Maxim* magazines.

Counting print, TV, and video exposure, millions of people view Tao every year. One recent program alone—the Teva Mountain Games coverage on Fox Television—was broadcast to 150 million households.

He's a public speaker sought by business audiences seeking lessons on risk taking and goal setting, and by schoolchildren keen to meet an extreme-sports celebrity.

Sports Illustrated writes, "Berman is the best-known kayaker on the planet," and *Rolling Stone* calls Tao the "world's most extreme paddler." His Web site is **www.taoberman.com.**

P am Withers is a longtime whitewater kayaker and author of thirteen teen adventure novels, most of them best-sellers and three of them award nominees. A former editor at *River World* and *Adventure Travel* magazines and a popular public speaker, she has written for publications ranging from the *New York Times* to *McCall's*. Her Web site is **www.takeittotheextreme.com.**

INDEX

DEAR CUSTOMERS AND FRIENDS,

SUPPORTING YOUR INTEREST IN OUTDOOR ADVENTURE, travel, and an active lifestyle is central to our operations, from the authors we choose to the locations we detail to the way we design our books. Menasha Ridge Press was incorporated in 1982 by a group of veteran outdoorsmen and professional outfitters. For 25 years now, we've specialized in creating books that benefit the outdoors enthusiast.

Almost immediately, Menasha Ridge Press earned a reputation for revolutionizing outdoors- and travel-guidebook publishing. For such activities as canoeing, kayaking, hiking, backpacking, and mountain biking, we established new standards of quality that transformed the whole genre, resulting in outdoor-recreation guides of great sophistication and solid content. Menasha Ridge continues to be outdoor publishing's greatest innovator.

The folks at Menasha Ridge Press are as at home on a white-water river or mountain trail as they are editing a manuscript. The books we build for you are the best they can be, because we're responding to your needs. Plus, we use and depend on them ourselves.

We look forward to seeing you on the river or the trail. If you'd like to contact us directly, join in at www.trekalong.com or visit us at www.menasharidge.com. We thank you for your interest in our books and the natural world around us all.

SAFE TRAVELS,

Bob Sehlinger

BOB SEHLINGER
PUBLISHER